Andy Moyle

Friends, Food and the Gospel

www.friendsfoodandthegospel.com

Friends, Food and the Gospel

Andy Moyle

First Printing: 2016

ISBN 978-1-326-74550-9

Published by The Gateway Church
99c High Street, King's Lynn, Norfolk PE30 1BW

Contents

Acknowledgements

I am profoundly grateful to so many people who have helped shape my life to make me a disciple of Jesus. I am loving the journey of Friends, Food and the Gospel.

The lovely Janet, who is a wonderful wife and the most hospitable person I know and love.

Our children, Rebecca, David and Katie, who have to put up with endless pizza parties and BBQs and a home full of laughter and people.

Mike Betts, Maurice Nightingale and Goff Hope from the Relational Mission Apostolic sphere of Newfrontiers. They took my crazy name for what they do so well and cheered us on in our adventure.

Tony Thompson, church planter extraordinaire and viral evangelist, who believed in me and encouraged me to plant churches.

Markus and Ellen Adolfsson who taught us how to do international food evenings in Rockneby, Sweden.

Jonathan and Nolda Tipping in Onnen, Netherlands who do "Friends, food and the Gospel" with refugees in their village.

The Gateway Church in King's Lynn where we are enjoying the adventure!

1

Introduction

To the weak I became weak, that I might win the weak. I have become all things to all people, that by all means I might save some. I do it all for the sake of the gospel, that I may share with them in its blessings. (1 Corinthians 9:22-23 ESV)

It took me five minutes to find the body. It was a cold dark night and moments before I had been driving to a youth leader's meeting on a winding country road. Now I was looking down at a dead young man. His lifeless eyes staring into mine as his chest heaved his dying breaths. A drunk driver had just swerved past me to overtake and ploughed into an oncoming motorcyclist as he passed. The drunk driver ended up in a ditch and was screaming, so I knew he was alive. The motorcyclist had been thrown into a farmer's field a long way and took some finding. As I looked into his lifeless eyes, I said out loud "Where have you just gone to?"

I didn't know where his ultimate destination would be. I found out later he was riding home from work back to his wife and two young daughters. But I didn't know where he had ended up. I didn't know whether anyone had taken the opportunity to let him know God loved him. To tell him that Jesus had died so that he could know God and have life to the full now and forever more.

In the horror of that moment, I knew I wanted to dedicate the rest of my life to planting churches and telling as many people as possible about the good news of Jesus Christ. There's an urgency to the Gospel – we never know what might happen, whether we will be here in ten minutes, ten days or ten years. I don't want anyone to die not knowing there's a God who loves them and died to prove it. The big question for me that night, nearly twenty years ago, was how?

Looking back over the last nearly two decades of church planting, we have learnt lots of lessons on how to make disciples through friendship and food. I'll confess. I'm not good at knocking on doors and I usually cringe at street drama and handing out tracts. I'm just not wired that way. Some are and bear great fruit. What I have found is that my wife and I love meeting people, making new friends and connecting them with our Christian friends over good food. We have found that relaxing over a simple meal, a pizza, jacket potatoes and fillings or a theme night, leads to deep friendship and a sense of family. We have discovered the art of team fishing, so that everyone gets to use their strengths working together, having fun and getting the Great Commission done.

> My wife and I love meeting people, making new friends and connecting them with our Christian friends over good food.

We do a lot of pizza parties, filling our garden with friends, cooking lots of pizza in a wood fired oven and then laughing and chatting in front of a fire pit to the sounds of jamming musicians. Those evenings have been the start of a journey for dear friends, often originally from distant nations, who have ended up becoming part of God's family and our family. Before everyone arrives I'm making my pizza sauce. I reduce chopped tomatoes, olive oil and garlic in a pan, simmering it until it is thick and flavoursome. In the same way, we have boiled our evangelistic strategy down to three essentials: Friends, Food and the Gospel.

This book contains some of the lessons and Biblical principles I have learnt along the way. Come with us and learn about team fishing, how you are wired to be part of the team, how to make friends, be hospitable and lead people to Christ and become disciples.

Friends, Food and the Gospel. Join us on the adventure…

2

Friends, Food and the Gospel

The Son of Man has come eating and drinking, and you say, 'Look at him! A glutton and a drunkard, a friend of tax collectors and sinners!' Yet wisdom is justified by all her children.' (Luke 7:34-35 ESV)

The importance of food

Food is important - not just for our energy needs, but what happens as we eat together with friends and family. I am a foodie! I love making food and eating food with friends. I love our big wooden kitchen table. I love how over steaming plates of pasta, deep conversations have happened, prophetic words have been given, the Gospel has been explained and lives have been transformed for eternity. A meal is as much about the people coming and the conversation, as it is about the food we have shared.

Meals were important in the life of Jesus too.

Tim Chester points out[i] there are three ways the Gospels complete the phrase "The Son of Man came to..."

1) The Son of Man came not to be served but to serve, and to give his life as a ransom for many (Mark 10:45);

2) The Son of Man came to seek and to save the lost (Luke 19:10);

3) The Son of Man has come eating and drinking (Luke 7:34).

The first two tell us what Jesus came to do – He came to seek out lost people and serve them by dying for them. The last one is the big shock. It tells us how He did it – Jesus came eating and drinking. The surprise is that the Jews were hoping for a Messiah, the "Son of Man" to use Daniel's term, who would overthrow the Romans in triumph and usher in a new age for Israel. They certainly did not expect him to come serving and seeking lost people and especially not the hated Gentiles. He was meant to come on the clouds as a mystical figure. Instead he came "eating and drinking" and doing that with the dregs of society, the tax collectors, loose women, the poor and the sick.

> "The Son of Man has come eating and drinking, and you say, 'Look at him! A glutton and a drunkard, a friend of tax collectors and sinners!'" (Luke 7:34)

What an accusation to make! Jesus must have been a party animal, eating and drinking with the people he came to serve, seek and save. Gluttons are people who eat too much. Drunkards drink too much. Jesus was serious about eating and drinking with people. Jesus was eating and drinking enough with the kinds of people who eat and drink too much to be accused of those things himself. Somehow he did it a lot, without sinning, so much so, that his enemies accused him of doing it to excess.

Earlier in Luke's Gospel we are told,

> The Pharisees and their scribes said to him, "The disciples of John fast often and offer prayers, and so do the disciples of the Pharisees, but yours eat and drink" (Luke 5:33).

Luke's gospel is essentially a journey towards the cross in Jerusalem, punctuated by meals. There were ten of them, recorded for us. In the Gospel, Jesus is either going to a meal, eating a meal or coming from a meal. It's a fantastic mission strategy. Jesus is calling us to a life of making friends, eating and sharing the Gospel with them, so they get to join the party and feast of The Kingdom of God.

The Kingdom of God is a feast

The feeding of the 5,000 in Luke 9 is a great story where we learn two key things. First of all, it is full of allusions to the Old Testament, to show who Jesus is and how the coming kingdom of God is a feast. Secondly Jesus wants us to take responsibility for doing His mission, knowing it is impossible. That means that we will have to rely on Him for empowering.

> *And he took them and withdrew apart to a town called Bethsaida. When the crowds learned it, they followed him, and he welcomed them and spoke to them of the kingdom of God and cured those who had need of healing. Now the day began to wear away, and the twelve came and said to him, "Send the crowd away to go into the surrounding villages and countryside to find lodging and get provisions, for we are here in a desolate place." But he said to them, "You give them something to eat." They said, "We have no more than five loaves and two fish—unless we are to go and buy food for all these people." For there were about five thousand men. And he said to his disciples, "Have them sit down in groups of about fifty each." And they did so, and had them all sit down. And taking the five loaves and the two fish, he looked up to heaven and said a blessing over them. Then he broke the loaves and gave them to the disciples to set before the crowd. And they all ate and were satisfied. And what was left over was picked up, twelve baskets of broken pieces. Luke 9:10-17*

Here are three key Old Testament allusions that show us who Jesus is.

1) Moses and the Manna

Hundreds of years before, God used Moses to rescue the people of Israel from slavery in Egypt. It didn't take them long to start complaining that they were hungry in the wilderness. So God gave them miraculous Manna, every day except on the Sabbath for forty years - *I am about to rain bread from heaven for you* Ex 16:4.

The 5,000 in the crowd listening to Jesus are also in a wilderness without food. Jesus looks up to heaven and again bread miraculously comes down. Jesus is thus the New Moses, who is about to lead the people to a New Exodus, which is freedom from slavery to sin.

2) Elijah and the feast for the prophets

The first century readers of the feeding of the 5000 would have been reminded of a second Old Testament story from 2 Kings 4:42-44. Elisha is with a group of prophets during a time of famine. Someone brings them their first fruits, twenty loaves of barley. Elisha tells his servant to feed a group of one hundred prophets with the 20 loaves. The servant asks "How can I?" Just like the twelves disciples in Luke 9, Elisha wants the servant to take responsibility for the miracle. So Elisha tells him, *"Give it to the men, that they may eat and have some left."*

Elisha's servant does it, so that the many are fed and there are leftovers. In Luke, Jesus does the same, telling his disciples to feed 5,000 with 5 loaves and two fishes. They protest. But they do it. There's not only enough, there are baskets of leftovers, 12 of them. This is symbolic of the feast of the kingdom starting and never ending.

When Elijah had been taken up to heaven, Elisha took his cloak and the mantle of his anointing, because he was the successor. Elisha is the New Elijah. The feeding of the 5,000 is telling us that because Jesus miracles are even greater than Elisha's, He is an even greater new Elijah.

Jesus is the New Moses and the New Elijah. Peter knows He is the Christ. That is brought out by the third Old Testament allusion.

3) Messianic banquet

800 years before Jesus came to the earth, Isaiah proclaimed

> *On this mountain the LORD of hosts will make for all peoples a feast of rich food, a feast of well-aged wine, of rich food full of marrow, of aged wine well refined. And he will swallow up on this mountain the covering that is cast over all peoples, the veil that is spread over all nations. He will swallow up death forever; and the Lord GOD will wipe away tears from all faces, and the reproach of his people he will take away from all the earth, for the LORD has spoken. It will be said on that day, "Behold, this is our God; we have waited for him, that he might save us. This is the LORD; we have waited for him; let us be glad and rejoice in his salvation." Isa 25:6-9*

That is a goose bump passage. Jesus, the Lord, is the Messiah who invites us to a Messianic banquet. A banquet where death has been abolished. Tears have been wiped away. Guilt, shame and fear have gone. The kingdom of God is a feast! A feast of rich food, good wine and meat! I want to see heaven manifested as much as possible on earth now, so what better way to see it grow than by feasting!

The feeding of the 5,000 establishes clearly who Jesus is – the New Moses, the New Elijah and the Messiah who invites us to His great feast in the kingdom of God.

Responsibility for the mission

When Jesus tells the disciples to feed the crowd, he is teaching them and us to take responsibility for the miracle and the mission. We know it is humanly impossible. We cannot feed thousands. We cannot save even one person, let alone thousands. So we have to rely on the power of God to get it done. Both Elisha and Jesus wanted their disciples to take responsibility for doing the miracle. In both situations they were told "You do it." Jesus and Elisha were not setting their followers up to fail. They were setting them up to be dependent on God who is the source of all power and authority. They both knew it was humanly impossible and would require their followers to exercise faith and reliance on God for the miracle. And in both cases their followers did just that.

We have an amazing mission, a Great Commission, to go into all the world and make disciples (Matt 28:19-20). It's an impossible task, one that we can't do on our own. One that will require us to work in teams and rely on the power of God to get it done. Let's unpack that in the next chapter.

3

Follow me and I will make you fishers of men

"Come follow me and I will make you fishers of men" Matt 4:19

Rod and Line Fishing

When people talk of fishing, we often think of middle aged men, exhausted from a week's work, living in a busy household, sat on the river bank for an afternoon's peace and quiet with a rod and line catching a few fish every now and again. Switch that with Middle Eastern subsistence fishermen 2000 years ago and you get a radically different picture.

> Team work makes the dream work

They worked as a team, because their livelihoods and their lives depended on it. Peter was boss, standing at the front. He knew where to go and watched out for shoals of fish to catch. James and John, nicknamed "sons of thunder", hoisted sails, cast nets and rowed hard. That is when they weren't arguing. I can see Andrew at the helm as Peter pointed where to go. Zebedee, the oldest, would often have been fast asleep snuggled in among the nets, ready to spring into action when needed.

Jesus said to them

"Come follow me and I will make you fishers of men" Matt 4:19

They would have instinctively worked together as a team, each playing to their strengths and covering one another's weaknesses. They would have used a nets approach not a rod and line approach.

In the West, we live in an individualistic culture and society. We naturally tend towards going it alone, reaching our friend on our own. Our individualistic lifestyles make it much harder to witness and affects our attitude to evangelism. Consequently there's a lot of guilt and pressure when it comes to what I call the "E-word", Evangelism. Here are two common scenarios.

Many churches are not outward looking at all. Every now and again, an evangelist stirs the people, who all feel guilty, so they organise a guest speaker or mission. Loads of work is done getting ready for the outreach and then not one non-believer turns up. Or a few do, pray a prayer and are then never seen again. Satisfied we have done our bit, everything can then return back to normal.

Another scenario is that "evangelism" is standing on a street corner preaching and handing out tracts. We've only been "evangelising" when we have given the four spiritual laws or done the bridge to life™ diagram with someone. Trouble with that is that not many of us are wired that way. I suspect that most of my church would rather have root canal work done at the dentist!

Team fishing is a much better approach.

Just as Peter, James, John, Andrew and Zebedee would have recognised they each had different strengths they could use, we need to do the same in our small groups particularly. The first myth to dispel is that we are only witnessing if we have shared the whole gospel and invited a response. As we will see in the next chapter becoming a disciple is a process. We all get to play a part in different stages of people's journey to faith and discipleship. Some befriend, maybe a couple have shared their story and someone else invites them to an event. A few people take the time to explain the Gospel with clarity and then one day the penny drops and someone leads them to Christ. As the Apostle Paul wrote to the Corinthians,

"I planted, Apollos watered, but God gave the growth." 1 Cor 3:6

I was so helped by Bill Hybel's "Becoming a Contagious Christian" twenty years ago, where he identified six Biblical styles of evangelism – interpersonal, invitational, testimonial, intellectual, serving and confrontational. It was a release to help people play to their strength to reach friends. I am unashamedly charismatic so I added a power style to Hybel's list of six. Over years of team fishing I have found that interpersonal people are usually invitational too, so I have tweaked the styles and renamed them to serve our cultural context better.

Here are the six different styles of evangelistic witnessing in operation in the pages of the New Testament and today – Connecting, Reasoning, Power, Serving, Storytelling and Harvesting.

In many churches, evangelism was just for the "Harvesters." Trans-local evangelists who equip local churches in evangelism are usually by nature Harvesters, training with Harvester only methods. If they forget the other styles, they will fail to mobilise the whole church family, who are not naturally Harvesters themselves.

Those of us who connect well with people, can explain and answer questions, are passionate about prophecy or healing, who love to serve people or tell their stories just did so inside the confines of the church family. They aren't using their gifts and talents to reach people in their work, leisure or market places, because no one has told them they can!

But when we fish as a team, everyone gets to use the way they are wired to be involved in the process of fishing with nets together. We all get to "do" evangelism together!

So what do the six styles look like and how do they relate to Friends, Food and the Gospel?

Connecting Style

Some people are just great at making friends and building community. In a later chapter we will see Levi excelling in this strength within the newly formed 12 disciples. If you are a connector, you'll have hundreds of friends on Facebook. You'll be the kind of person who knows everybody's birthdays and remember details about people's lives.

Malcolm Gladwell in the excellent book Tipping Point, came up with the term Connector. Most people have a few close friends and family. Connectors often have hundreds of loose connections with people.

They instinctively know how to connect the right people with each other. They will introduce Bob who has some deep questions with Fred who has a Reasoning style of evangelism. They will hook Anna, a new mum with Sarah who has just moved to the area with a new born baby.

Appendix 1 contains a UK version of Gladwell's surname test that he uses as an easy way to see if you are a Connector. The idea is you quickly note down the number of people you know with each surname listed – Connectors will score hundreds!

Connectors are often also brilliant at inviting people to things! The Samaritan woman at the well in John 4 is a good example. She actually had three things going against her for being a connector in her setting. She was a Samaritan, she was a woman and she was an adulteress. That doesn't stop Jesus from talking to her and using questions prompted by a word of knowledge to cut to the heart of her need of Christ. Even with the stigma of her previous lifestyle, she then runs back to her village to invite them all to meet Jesus and they come! If you are a connector like her, you connect, no matter how tough your current situation is.

One of our junior doctors is a great Connector. She has been amazing at inviting people to small group parties in the first year she has been with us - we now have four other junior doctors attending church, one of whom became a Christian a few months ago.

The first large event we held when we were planting our current church was a Chinese food buffet and charity auction. We had around 30 people at the time attending and somehow 150 people turned up to the event. It turned out that 90 of the guests were invited by just two families – so we were quickly able to work out how our Connectors were!

A further example of the power of Connectors in team fishing is shown by some Tearfund[ii] funded research into churchgoing in the UK. They interviewed people who don't go to church regularly to find out what, if anything, would prompt them to give it a go! The staggering result is that 28% of people who don't go to church, but are open to spiritual things, would come to a Sunday meeting *if invited*. Even 6% of people totally closed to church would come if invited. The percentages would be clearly much higher if invited to a small group BBQ.

In the research, people that don't go to church regularly were interviewed and then put into six categories.

1. Fringe people are on the fringe of the church community.
2. Occasional people go occasionally, perhaps once a month or for festivals.
3. Open de-churched are people that used to go to church and still open to the Christian Faith.
4. Open non-churched are people that have never gone to church and are open to the Christian faith.
5. Closed de-churched are people that used to go to church and are now closed to the Christian faith.
6. Closed non-churched have never been to church and are not interested.

The table below shows us the incredible power of Connectors ability to make friends who don't know Jesus and invite them.

	Fringe	Occasional	Open de-churched	Open non-churched	Closed de-churched	Closed non-churched
Family member starts going	23%	18%	23%	15%	9%	4%
Invited personally	12%	13%	12%	28%	7%	6%
Friend starts going	12%	9%	13%	8%	5%	2%

When you match the Connectors' ability to make new friends and bring them together with people reflecting the other 5 styles to eat, then the fireworks start!

Storytelling Style

When looking at John 4, what got the villagers convinced that Jesus is the Messiah? Verse 39 gives us the answer:

> *"Many Samaritans from that town believed in him because of the woman's testimony, 'He told me everything that I ever did.'"*

Combining a Storyteller sharing what happened to them with Jesus using word of knowledge meant a village starting to follow Jesus. Storytellers are great at telling stories of how God has worked in their lives.

The blind man who was healed by Jesus in John 9 had to immediately tell his story to a hostile audience. Interestingly he refused to get into a theological debate with them,

> *"Whether he (Jesus) is a sinner or not, I do not know. One thing I do know, that though I was blind, now I see."*

Those listening would have loved to have beaten him in a debate. A personal story cannot so easily be refuted. There is power in personal testimony, in storytelling.

In verse 3 we are told that he had been blind from birth so that the work of God could be displayed in his life. His life history made him perfect to be a storytelling witness.

Stories are powerful. Even ordinary stories. Actually, let me correct that - especially ordinary stories! We once had the "Beast of the North East", Davey Falcus, come to our church to tell his story of coming to faith and ministry out of his old life of being a gangster. He was fantastic! So often speakers with fantastic testimonies wow us. But people could argue they really needed Christ. Your ordinary story of finding Jesus in the midst of ordinary life relates to the people God has put you around, which can be just as powerful.

If you are a Storyteller, work on your personal faith story. When you are in conversation with people, you can tell your story of coming to faith or how God helped you through various situations.

When it comes to personal testimony, it's good to have different versions for different situations at your fingertips. The 30 second version is for that mid conversation question. As a church leader, I love it when I get asked "What do you do for a living?" Usually, I have 30 seconds to say something before their eyes glaze over. I want to say something that leads to another next question!

A 3min version of your testimony is helpful too, when someone asks you why you go to church. You can tell them what you were like before you became a Christian, the process of exploring Christianity leading to you deciding to follow Jesus and what it's like now.

Practice these different versions of your story without jargon – see if you can do it without the words 'blessed' and 'sin', for example. You need to cover the concepts, but using words common to ordinary non-Christians!

Storytellers don't just tell their conversion story, but also personal things God has done, how He helped through difficulties. Anything that relates to what a friend is telling you they are going through, can have powerful impact. Make sure you listen to your friend fully. Don't interrupt with your me-too, midway through their story. That's irritating!

Serving Style

Others are servant hearted. They love to help others. Within the framework of Friends, Food and the Gospel, the Servants are key team players. They are the ones who make the food that goes to people's hearts! The success of pizza parties as an evangelistic social is largely down to the servant hearted people who make sometimes dozens of pizzas in an evening with smiles on their faces and flour on their t-shirts.

Servants find it easy to serve people, because that is how God has wired them. They spot needs a mile off and love meeting them, even if they don't get credit.

> Servant hearted people who make sometimes dozens of pizzas in an evening with smiles on their faces and flour on their t-shirts.

In the New Testament, Dorcas became known to the disciples because of her acts of service (Acts 9:36-43). When she died lots of people came and showed the disciples what she had done for them. Peter raised her from the dead and many believed in the Lord. That's not to say a servant has to die before anyone will become a Christian through their servant-heartedness! It can be the slowest style, but teamed up with others, it's powerful.

St Francis of Assisi once said "Preach the gospel, use words if you have to." That's a terrible quote, because Romans 10:14-17 makes it clear people won't respond to the Gospel unless it contains the words of Christ. If you have servanthood as your main style, then make sure you tell people it is because God loves them that you are serving them.

Reasoning Style

When Paul was in Athens in Acts 18, he used a reasoning style of evangelism. He persuaded by argument the truth of the Gospel.

The apostle Paul had spotted Athens was a very religious city, with many statues and altars to the many gods worshipped there. One was to "The Unknown God", so Paul used persuasive arguments to show that the unknown god is actually Jesus who died for them and commands repentance. That caused mocking, interest and some new believers.

People with the reasoning style love the Scripture in 1 Peter 3:15

> *"Always be prepared to give an answer to everyone who asks you to give the reason for the hope that you have. But do this with gentleness and respect."*

Reasoners study answers to the main questions people have and are always ready to answer questions. The second part of the verse is really important – answer with gentleness and respect. Discussions can and do get pretty heated. The trouble with that is you may win the argument but lose a soul. You want to leave people thinking not simmering.

My friend, Carl Maidment, was frustrated that some of his friends didn't become Christians on an Alpha Course. He visited them and asked them why not. They answered that he hadn't answered their questions. So he found out what their questions were and that became the basis for the Christianity Unwrapped Course. It uses the values that makes Alpha a success – food, talks, discussion and the power of the Spirit, but starts at a lower level. Does God exist? And goes through the common questions until the only logical conclusion is that Christianity is the way to know God.

Harvesting Style

Most people's concept of the evangelist is the actually just one of these six styles we can spot in the New Testament – the Harvester. Most people therefore avoid evangelism completely because they are uncomfortable with confronting people with the Gospel and calling for a response. However what we really need is all the styles working together in team to be effective at reaching the most people.

In the Gospels, Peter is a pretty direct guy – always the first to get stuck in or just open his mouth. He also ended up as the one clearly explaining the Gospel and inviting response on the day of Pentecost.

Where others might find it hard to articulate the gospel and invite someone to cross the line of faith, people with the Harvesting style never shy away from doing this. They look for ways to clearly articulate the gospel – the bridge to life, the four spiritual laws, do vs done and the Roman road and are ready to use an appropriate method in conversation and speaking.

Sometimes they need to temper their full on nature and make sure they are flowing with the same compassion Jesus has. I remember running an Alpha in the very early days of our church and asked the one guest most weeks, to my wife's chagrin, are you ready to cross the line of faith yet?

Power

The last style has experienced a renaissance in the last few decades. This is where people rely on the utterance charismatic gifts, prophecy, word of knowledge, word of wisdom and miracles to witness to unbelievers the goodness and power of God.

Prophetic evangelism, treasure hunting, healing on the streets are all methodologies that have allowed prophetically gifted people to exercise spiritual gifts with not yet believers.

It was a dominant style in the setting of the Acts of the Apostles. Most of the evangelistic and church planting breakthroughs in the book of Acts kicked off with a miracle, followed by gospel proclamation (see Acts 2:1-41; 3:1-26; 5:12-16; 8:4-8; 9:32-35; 9:32-35; 9:36-43; 13:9-12; 14:3; 16:27-31; 19:11-12; 20:7-12 and 29:1-10)

Prophetic evangelism seeks to use prophetic revelation with not yet believers. I love it when people tell me their dreams – I ask God for the interpretation and then give it. God loves to speak and 1 Cor 14 tells us that

> *"If an unbeliever enters a place where we are prophecying then he is convicted by all, he is held to account by all, the secrets of his heart are disclosed and so falling on his face, he will worship God".*

As I was growing in prophetic confidence, I remember getting a very specific word of knowledge about a lonely lady sitting on a sofa during the previous Thursday evening, waiting desperately for the phone to ring, but it didn't. This story is pre Facebook! The only way you can find out if you are hearing God or making it up, is to step out and speak it out. As I shared the word of knowledge, I could see a lady on the back row sinking in her chair, hiding as I described her Thursday evening in detail. Not long after that she became a Christian.

Some people with the Power style go treasure hunting. This is about looking for the treasure that God wants to bless on the streets. Treasure hunters spend a few minutes asking God for some clues like clothing, location, names and ailments and then go out with their treasure map to look for people to bless, prophecy over and heal.

Another favourite of Power style people is Healing on the Streets, which started in my wife's home town of Coleraine. During a H.O.T.S session, chairs are set out and healing prayer is offered – hundreds have been healed and thousands saved in the last 20 years.

People who operate with the power style love praying for the sick, and seek God for prophetic insight for people they come into contact with.

Team work makes the dream work

Working as a team, where everyone uses the styles they are most comfortable helps to break the unhelpful individualistic approach of the western world. We stop struggling with a rod and line and start casting our nets together.

When we work as a team, my friends become your friends. Resistance to being outward looking begins to evaporate. Those that don't have many or any non-Christian friends get to meet the friends of Connectors. We also pray together as part of the witness section of our small group evening. Team work makes the dream work!

When I was working at The Open Door Church in St Neots in the late 90's I remember a testimony where a newly converted couple said they knew Tony and he was nice. But when they got to meet Tony's small group and found that they were all nice, they began to realise the commonality of niceness was the Christian faith. That got them interested and asking questions.

The first people to become Christians through our Friends, Food and the Gospel strategy were two Chinese students working for a year in a local high school. One of them said, "I met the small group and you were all so nice. I wanted what you had." The other said, "I visited some art galleries and all the art was Christian scenes and that got me interested in Jesus and so when I met you all, I started asking questions."

The Connectors have lots of friends and begin to introduce them to other people in the small group, so that they begin to become part of the wider community of the small group or church. That way, when they are invited to a social event or a guest service, they already know some people.

There is nothing more frightening for most people than going somewhere new where you don't know anybody. I still remember when my parents dropped me off at the halls of residence of the university I went to. I sat in my room for a few moments, like everyone else, nervous. And then I got up and knocked on doors and put the kettle on.

If people already know some other people who are going to an event then it's not such a hurdle for them to go too. Tony Thompson, who used to lead The Open Door Church in St Neots, tells the story of being invited to a neighbour's evening wedding anniversary BBQ when he first moved there. Throughout the day people were arriving, so he kept checking the invite and then looking through the curtains, nervously. He's a gregarious extrovert, but he was wondering why people were there already. At the appointed hour Tony and his wife Anne took a deep breath and walked across the street. Within minutes all the other neighbours who had been feeling and doing the same, joined them at the party!

They then found out the earlier guests were all wider family members.

So the Connectors make and bring friends, the Servants make the social food gathering happen, the Reasoners may get to answer some questions, Storytellers may get to tell their story, Power folks might get the opportunity to pray for healing and eventually the Harvesters will get to share the gospel, perhaps scribbled on the back of an envelope. It can and should all happen very naturally!

Team work makes the dream work and means we fish for men and women with nets, not a rod and line. It's also a lot more fun, less pressured and naturally supernatural.

Application

1) In your small group discuss which styles you all are. If some are lacking, look to gather them into your group.

2) Start to plan ways that some of the friends of people in the group can become friends of the group. Be creative!

Making Disciples

Go therefore and make disciples of all nations, baptizing them in the name of the Father and of the Son and of the Holy Spirit, teaching them to observe all that I have commanded you. And behold, I am with you always, to the end of the age.' (Matthew 28:19-20 ESV)

Go and make disciples

Before putting team fishing in practice, we need to know what we are trying to achieve. The great commission of Matt 28:19-20 makes it clear our calling is to go into all the world and make disciples. A disciple is someone who is actively following Jesus – I am far more interested in counting new disciples than new professions of faith. Someone can pray "the prayer" on the streets or at an altar call and you never see them again. That may be because they were a visitor and they go on to follow Jesus back home. But often "the prayer" is little more than the protestant version of the absolution with little, if any follow up and no on-going evidence of repentance and faith.

The parable of the sower illustrates this perfectly. The new disciple is the one who is like good soil, accepting the Gospel and growing to produce fruit. Mere professors can be like seeds on the rock, with no foundations. They can also be like seed on a path, where it doesn't take long for the devil to snatch the word away. Or like thorny soil, soon choked by the cares of the world.

> Counting professions breeds cynicism

Counting professions breeds cynicism because often they are never seen again. I'm not convinced it's a Biblical idea anyway! The 3,000 in Acts 2 were saved and added. The "added" changes the scenario from a profession of faith to a life. It changes it to a relationship with Jesus and devotion to the local church family.

In the New Testament, becoming a disciple is made up of four strands – like legs of a chair. You need four chair legs for long term stability.

Repentance

Repentance comes from the Greek word *metanoeo* which means to change one's mind. It's to realise that we have been going our way, thinking and acting our thoughts and not God's. On a general level, it is realising that God's way is better than my way. That God's good is so much better than our good. Isaiah 64:6 describes our human righteous acts as a menstrual cloth and in Phil 3:8 as human excreta. Self-righteous acts are those efforts to earn favour by our own righteousness. God finds them as offensive as crude sin. Knowing that is the beginning of repentance.

Thinking leads to speaking. Realising that God's way is better than ours leads to confession of that audibly. The mouth is the channel of communication between the outside and inside.

"For by your words you will be justified and by your words you will be condemned" (Matt 12:37)

"What comes out of a person is what defiles him. For from within our of the heart of man, come evil thoughts, sexual immorality, theft, murder, adultery, coveting, wickedness, deceit, sensuality, envy, slander, pride, foolishness. All these evil things come from within and they defile a person" Mark 7:20-23

Evil starts in our hearts and flows out of our mouths and other body parts as we sin. Therefore repentance which starts in the heart as a thinking change also needs to flow out of our mouths in confession. We name specific things rather than a vague "I must have sinned some time" – "I did this... and this... and this..." As those words come out, pride is swallowed! Alongside that is renunciation – as a schoolboy put it "Sorry enough to stop!"

Thinking flows to speaking which then flows to deed. Part of John the Baptist's frustration was that while he was on message with repentance, he couldn't offer the power of the Spirit for on-going changed lives. That frustration came out in Luke 3:8:

"You brood of vipers, produce fruit in keeping with repentance!"

Zacchaeus was a great example of deeds flowing from repentance. He not only stopped ripping people off in the future, but he paid back those he had defrauded in the past. The Ephesian ex-occultists burned their occult books.

This turning to God means that He turns to us too!

Repent therefore, and turn back, that your sins may be blotted out, that times of refreshing may come from the presence of the Lord, and that he may send the Christ appointed for you, Jesus (Acts 3:19-20)

Faith

Faith is incredibly important to becoming a new disciple. That's because grace gives and faith takes!

"For by grace you have been saved through faith. And this is not your own doing, it is the gift of God, not a result of works, so that no one may boast." Eph 2:8-9

The simplest answer to "what must I do to be saved?" is "Believe in the Lord Jesus and you will be saved." Acts 16:30-31. Faith must be spoken out. *"If you confess with your mouth that Jesus is Lord and believe in your heart that God raised Him from the dead, you will be saved."* (Romans 10:9) It's not just saying we have faith that saves us, it is having it!

What do we believe? This short list about Jesus Christ would seem to me to be enough...

- Jesus is the Son of God and our Lord.

- Jesus died on the cross for our sin

- Jesus rose again bodily, defeating sin, death and the devil.

Repentance and faith are the basic essentials to eternal life. The thief on the cross who realised he deserved to die and Jesus didn't was expressing repentance. Asking Jesus to remember Him in paradise was expressing faith in Him. "Truly I say to you, today you will be with me in paradise" is Jesus telling him he has eternal life on those two legs – repentance and faith.

Obviously being nailed to a cross, to die in a matter of hours, would prevent one from being able to get the other two legs of becoming a disciple.

Baptism in Water

Baptism in water is a physical act that has spiritual effects. The other three legs all include physical elements too alongside the spiritual. Repentance may involve clothes (Luke 3:11), money (Luke 9:8) and books (Acts 19:19). Faith involves the mouth – Romans 10:9 makes speaking out essential to being saved. Baptism in Spirit comes generally through the laying on of hands. The book of Acts shows it typically has physical manifestations of tongues, praise and/or prophecy.

The Greek view of man splits us into three – spirit, soul (mind, will and emotions) and body. The Hebraic view is much more a unity – oneness. Three in one! We are after all made in the image of God, the trinity, who is three in one. The physical is therefore part and parcel of the spiritual.

> Perhaps the best translation of baptizo is pickle!

Jesus gave us two physical acts with spiritual significance to do – baptism at the start of becoming a disciple and the Lord's supper going on.

The word baptise, is a transliteration of the Greek word baptizo. Essentially we have anglicised the word, rather than translating it. That is because the meaning of baptizo is a bit of a mouthful. Baptizo literally means to dip, drench or immerse with a sense of a change of identity occurring. I can understand transliterating it to "baptise."

35

The Greek word, *baptizo*, was a normal one too, not just religious one like baptise. A cloth is dyed, by baptising it in the dye. An onion is pickled by baptising it in vinegar. So perhaps the best translation of baptizo is pickle! The idea is of total immersion, with a change of identity happening. That's why baptism by sprinkling misses the point and spiritual imagery of full immersion. It's baptism "in" not "with" or the word loses its meaning.

The physical act of baptising someone in water has so much spiritual significance.

- It is a burial for those who are dead. Going down into the water signifies our old self dying to come up again, risen as a new creation in Christ.

- It is a bath for those who are dirty, symbolising the washing away of sins and our conscience cleansed. 1 Pet 3:21.

- It is a public act to consummate repentance and communicate forgiveness has happened.

Baptism in Spirit

John the Baptist found out that his baptism dealt with the past but gave no guarantees or power for the future. So when Jesus came to him to be baptised, John cried out *"He will baptise you with the Holy Spirit and with power."* We don't just need a pickling in water, we need the baptism in Spirit too. Many evangelicals believe that receiving the Spirit is automatic and imperceptible on repenting and believing. They confuse the regenerating work of the Spirit with receiving the power of Spirit. Regeneration is the work of the Spirit to make us born again. Regeneration makes our spirit which was dead because of sin alive in Christ. Regeneration opens our spirit to repent and believe. The baptism in Spirit is different. It is a filling with power to be a witness, receive the gifts and begin growing fruit.

After centuries of such confusion, it is contentious to suggest a dear, holy Christian, who loves the Lord, needs the fourth basic leg of baptism in Spirit after all. When I was 17 I bought my first car, a Morris Minor. I drove it happily for months, before someone pointed out that rather raspy engine sound was because I was running it on three not four cylinders. After a few days' work, it was firing on all four cylinders! That's what the baptism in Spirit does – empowers us to be a four cylinder Christian!

Reading through the book of Acts shows us how it works. In all the accounts, bar two, the baptism in Spirit happens when someone lays hands on someone else – a sense of imparting the Spirit. The two unique situations where that didn't happen were at Pentecost, where there was no-one to do it yet and Cornelius the Gentile, because no Jewish believer would touch him to lay hands on him.

Generally some form of outward physical manifestation happens as an overflow of the infilling of the Spirit. I'm not as dogmatic as my Pentecostal friends on the gift of tongues being the only acceptable initial evidence. But then I didn't have to fight for it! In the book of Acts, there is also praise and prophecy. The accounts of baptism in Spirit in the book of Acts show that it comes with some sort of physical overflow of what is going on in the Spirit, usually involving utterance. The Apostle Paul isn't recorded as initially speaking in tongues. Scales fell off his eyes, so he could see again. Eventually he is known as the one who speaks in tongues more than anyone. But the Biblical evidence for initial evidence having to be tongues just isn't there. Some people get the gift of tongues straight away, some bubble over with praise and others start to prophecy. That said I always look for people to receive the gift of tongues, either as we pray or later in the privacy of their own home. The Apostle Paul considered it such a personally helpful gift that he wrote of his hope that all would use it in 1 Cor 14:5.

So there you have the four legs of becoming a disciple – repentance, faith, baptism in water and baptism in Spirit. Before we get to look at making disciples through friends, food and the Gospel we needed to know what we are looking to make!

Becoming a disciple is a process

It is well worth reading through the book of Acts, not just to see how the baptism in Spirit happened, but to look at all the examples of people becoming a disciple. As you put the stories together you will find all four legs are a necessary for becoming a disciple. Not every account has all four, as that would be boring and repetitious. In fact in each one, only the striking legs are mentioned to build the narrative.

> The velocity is less important than the validity!

So for example, in Acts 2, Peter mentions repentance, baptism in water and Spirit, but not faith, which is implied in the questions and the fact they received the word.

Acts 8 only mentions the Ethiopian Eunuch getting baptised in water. That's the exciting bit. As a Eunuch he wasn't allowed into the Temple (Deuteronomy 23:1-3), but he is allowed to be baptised!

In Acts 9 Paul is baptised in water and receives the Spirit. There is no mention of repentance and faith – although both are clearly implied.

There's a process from repenting to receiving the Spirit, which for some was quick and some quite long. The twelve apostles took some years, the Ephesians disciples months, the Samaritan converts a couple of weeks, the Apostle Paul a few days, the Philippian jailer a few hours and Cornelius' family a few minutes. As David Pawson put it "The velocity is less important than the validity!" In many of the church planting situations in Acts, the first thing the following apostles did was ensure all four legs were solidly in place. The first question Paul asked the Ephesians (Acts 18) was did you receive the Spirit when you believed? Because it is not usually automatic, so the question needed to be asked. In the ensuing discussion he discovers they haven't believed in Jesus fully or been baptised either!

So far I have illustrated the process that a new disciple goes through as they become ready to come to faith. Before that is a longer process. I often use this pyramid to show the process and journey people go through to come to Jesus, especially when a relational methodology like Friends, Food and the Gospel is used. The pyramid represents the entire population. The size of each segment reflects the differing numbers of people at each stage.

Don't know any Christians

At the bottom, the largest segment is those people around us who
don't know any Christians at all. In the UK context, that is a lot of
people. In the 21st Century that means they will have no concept of
who Jesus is either. They may be open to friendship with a
Christian though and so the next segment up is made up of people
who are open to friendship. The fascinating thing here is that if we
fish using rod and line thinking, you may be the only Christian they
know. You must be a nice person (especially as you have read this
far!), but they may not equate your being nice with your faith. When
we fish as a team and your friend gets to know your group of
Christian friends and they are all as nice as you, the penny begins to
drop. The Christian faith is the common denominator with your
niceness! We experienced this a couple of years ago, when a
Chinese student mentioned in an earlier chapter became a Christian.

Open to friendship

People at the "Open to friendship" stage are watching. They are watching the welcome, how we interact with each other, how we love one another, especially the odd people. They are observing disciples loving one another and are finding it attractive. Jesus gave this instruction:

> *"A new command I give you: Love one another. As I have loved you, so you must love one another. By this everyone will know that you are my disciples, if you love one another." (John 13:35)*

There is something so attractive about the loving way Christians do life. The Apostle Paul described it as the aroma of Christ (2 Corinthians 2:14-16). To some people it's the smell of life, to others it's the smell of death. Some people find they like the smell of Christians. Others, blinded by the enemy, or smarting from previous interactions find it a stench.

Open to the message

Some friends who have become embedded in the friendship circle of a small group, enjoying the meals and socials become "open to the message." Jesus describes them as men and women of peace in Luke 10:6. There is something of the peace of God about them. Your peace has rested on them.

There are a number of ways to recognise a man or woman of peace. In Luke 10 Jesus tells the disciple to **look** for the man of peace. There's always someone that has an openness to the kingdom in a people group. Theologian Thom Wolf says a person of peace can be recognised by one of these 3R's

i)   They are *receptive* to the Gospel;

ii)   They possess a *reputation* to gain attention for the
        message among family and community;

iii)   They effectively *refer* the bearers of good news to that
        larger group.[iii]

I love how US pastor Naeem Fazal puts it *"Evangelism is joining the conversation God is already having with a person. You don't meet someone to talk to by accident. God is committed to them already."* [iv] I love that quote, it's so helpful and it takes the pressure off!

Not all men and women of peace will come to faith, some of them will be people of goodwill who introduce us to others who do! Janet had a young man working with her as a teaching assistant who was like that. He has personally never shown any interest in the Gospel or coming to Church but has introduced us to other family members who have!

At this stage the Reasoning style people, Storytellers and Harvesters will be active, asking and answering questions and sharing stories. The Power people may well have a word of knowledge that is the key to unlocking the friend's heart.

Ready

Friends start by watching and they watch the disciples loving one another. There comes a point where they find they are no longer just watching, they are now searching. There are questions being asked and answers being searched for. After a while there comes a point where they are no longer searching, they are actively seeking. God promises that He will be found when we seek Him with all our heart. They are ready, ready to cross the line of faith. To put their trust in Jesus Christ as Lord and Saviour. Often at this point a

Harvester in our team fishing concept uses his or her gifting and anointing to help bring someone through.

Disciple

Of course we are not just looking for professions of faith we are looking to make disciples. To help friends repent and put their faith in Jesus, to be baptised in water and in Spirit and go on to walk in the Spirit and get involved in local church life and team fishing.

In the next chapters we will look at how Friends, Food and the Gospel works in practice to team fish and make disciples.

Application

1 How did you get all four legs of becoming a disciple in place?

2 What friends do you have at the various levels – open to the friendship, open to the message and ready?

3 What opportunities can you plan to mix your Christian and non-Christian friends together?

5

Making Friends

It is not good for the man to be alone. (Gen 2:18 ESV)

An epidemic of loneliness

Britain is the 3rd loneliest country in Europe according to the Office for National Statistics. Some five million people have no close friends.^v Loneliness has long been recognised and worked on for older people, but recent research is showing an epidemic of friendlessness among younger people. You'd think with Facebook "friends" that people would have lots of friends, but the reverse seems to be true.

God the model of relationship, created us for relationship.

It is not good for the man to be alone. Gen 2:18

We were created to be social beings, not islands. We were made with a need for friends and the desire to enjoy warm, healthy and lasting friendships with others. The fundamental issue that hinders friendships is of course the sin that separates from God and from each other. The Gospel wonderfully reconciles us to God and one another. We have seen how Jesus beautifully models friendship. He is a friend of sinners, continually eating with tax collectors and sinners. He is the one who says of His disciples,

No longer do I call you servants, for the servant does not know what his master is doing; but I have called your friends... John 15:15

Friendship thus became a glorious hallmark of the early church, who were devoted to fellowship. Jesus promise *By this all people will know that you are my disciples, if you have love for one another (John 13:35)* was so thoroughly obvious to the Jewish historian Josephus, that he wrote "See how these Christians love one another."

So clearly we are called to be friends with our brothers and sisters in the church and those who are not yet part of the family.

Levels of friendship

There are levels of friendship. Jesus was friendly to the crowd, knew the 72 better, had 12 close followers, 3 inner circle and John his closest friend. We can represent the different levels of friendship and their depth of intimacy on this graph.

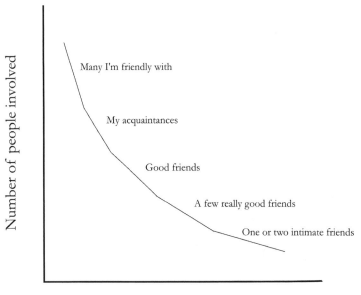

Depth of friendship

No friends at all

It is of course possible to be off the scale, with no friends at all. King David had a season like that which he describes:

> *Look to my right and see, no-one is concerned for me. I have no refuge; no one cares for my life Psalm 142:4*

Jesus, the model of friendship was also totally abandoned by his friends, prophecied by Isaiah, "He was despised and rejected by men; a man of sorrows and familiar with suffering." Isa 53:3. If you're in this state, Jesus identifies with you, is your most reliable friend and will empower you to find friends too.

Many people I am friendly with

Just like Jesus interacted with crowds, there will be many people we interact with you on a daily or weekly basis – cashiers, the newsagent, the petrol pump attendant, the gym receptionist and the parents dropping off children at the school gate.

Acquaintances

Jesus had the 72 who were closer. These are the people you know the first name of and will pass conversation with me. My 16 year old daughter's thousand Facebook "friends" will be in this category too!

Good friends

Jesus picked the twelve "he desired" (Mark3:13) to be good friends. You'll know your good friend's birthdays and will be in contact frequently!

A few really good friends

Jesus had the three – Peter, James and John that he took with him to the mount of transfiguration. These are the friends you look forward to spending an evening with and would drop everything to help solve a middle of the night crisis.

One or two intimate friends

John describes himself as the disciple that Jesus loved. There's clearly a special friendship between Jesus and John, who was asked to look after Mary, Christ's mother.

A healthy relational life operates at all levels on the scale. Introverts may feel more comfortable at the more intimate levels and extroverts at the less intimate. However we can work on all levels.

How do we make friends?

Be friendly

The best way to get friends is to be a friend. The starting point is to be friendly to everyone we can. We can cast seeds of friendship widely just by being friendly and in doing some find men and women of peace open to friendship and even the message. Smiling goes a long way!

Being respectful and courteous

Those values go a long way. Respect is putting a high value on others, regarding them as valuable. Opening the door for people, letting someone go ahead of you in a queue are simple courtesies.

When you encounter someone for the first time...

    i)   Aim to be the first to speak, to say hello.

ii) Look them in the eye and smile.

iii) Ask their name and use it a couple of times in the conversation. That's how I lock people's names to their faces, for when we meet again!

iv) Learn to ask questions – I was a quite lonely teenager. As I grew up, I learnt the art of small talk through asking questions. People love to talk about themselves so ask some questions.

v) Share something of yourself too.

Be helpful

"Hey, can you help me move flats?" It's a question we get asked every now and again. A friend calls and asks for help moving – because mum can't do heavy lifting and a removal company is too expensive. Friends help. Offering to help anytime it is needed and ask for help when you need are simple steps that develop friendships!

The early Christians in Acts enjoyed the favour of the people – given that they shared their time, money, possessions and life with those in need, in other words being helpful, means that is no surprise.

Be available.

Being a friendly person takes time and availability. Different levels of friendships call for varying degrees of availability. One of things African cultures have over Western culture is that they value people more than they value start times! When an African is "late", they have probably met someone along the way and spent time with them.

Jack Deere writes on availability of friends in "Surprised by the Voice of God"

> *Years ago I was in the process of developing a close friendship with a person who eventually became one of my closest friends. I was going through a difficult time and needed his help. As I was saying goodbye after lunch one day I asked him how late I could call him that night. He said I could call him as late as I wanted to. I told him I didn't want to wake him up, so I needed to know what time he planned to go to sleep. Then he said to me "It doesn't make any difference what time I go to sleep tonight. For you I am a twenty four hour friend, seven days a week. Call me whenever you want. I'll be there." You see, availability is one of the primary characteristics of friendships. Friends are available to their friends.*

Different levels of friendship have different levels of availability. It takes a deep friendship to be free to call me at 3am! Some might just have my office number, or email address.

Ask good questions

Asking open ended questions is a great way to get to know people. An open question invites more than a yes or no answer. "Did you have a good weekend?" is a closed question. "What did you do at the weekend?" invites a response!

There's a bit of an art to asking questions – I distinctly remember Jan and I going for dinner with a couple we were making friends with who asked loads of questions. They were really good at questioning, they got us talking and pushed a few buttons so got us sharing. But, we came away thinking they know us, but we know nothing about them at all. Conversations require a two and fro of questions and answering.

Start with the superficial and move deeper as you sense the comfort level increasing. "Do you think it will rain next week?" is so superficial that your new friend may wonder if you are interested in them at all. "What's your deepest darkest secret?" is going to make 99% of people really uncomfortable!

Be a listener

Film producer Ed Cunningham wrote *"Friends are those rare people who ask how we are, and then wait to hear the answer."* Being a listener is a really important quality for making friends. Most of us interrupt within 7 seconds, with something like:

"Oh I know what you mean. I.."

"Are you serious? I would have..."

"I can relate. I just had this happen..."

Being a good listener, is a hard skill to learn. For starters, nod instead of interrupting! When they have finished you can then reflect back – "That sounds like a tough day", "What a great story, hilarious!"

Jesus warns us *"Pay attention to what you hear, with the measure you use, it will be measured to you and still more will be added to you."* Mark 4:24

Some of the measures we need to be careful of are...

Listening for faults Matthew 7:1-2 *"Judge not, that you will not be judged. For with the judgement you pronounce you will be judged, and with the measure you use it will be measure to you."*

Be careful of adopting a cynical or judgemental attitude to others. Listen with compassion.

51

Listening to gossip. The trouble with gossip is it is so attractive, but it has a devastating effect.

> *The words of a whisperer are like delicious morsels; they go down into the inner parts of the body. (Proverbs 18:8 ESV)*

Words spoken about someone else go deep and it's hard to clear them out. We need to make a conscious decision not to listen and even risk unpopularity by speaking back positive things about the victim of the gossip.

Barriers to making friends

King Saul in the Old Testament doesn't appear to have had many friends. He couldn't trust people to get close and even argued with his son Jonathan, trying to kill him. As a lonely old man he made a desperate, but evil attempt to call up Samuel from the dead and ended up committing suicide.

Saul's first encounter with Samuel was incredible. Samuel prophecied over him about an encounter he would have with a group of prophets: "Then the Spirit will rush upon you, and you will prophecy with them and be turned into another man." 1 Sam 10:6. That's a picture of New Covenant Christianity where we are filled with the Spirit who changes us from the inside and gives us all the ability to hear God ourselves. Sadly Saul didn't build on that encounter with the help of strong friends. When he was under pressure he had no-one to turn to, to walk with him. There are six hindrances Saul had to deep friendships.

Self sufficiency

When the Philistines attached in 1 Samuel 13, Saul didn't wait for Samuel to make a sacrifice, but took matters into his own hands and made it himself.

Jesus told us without him we can do nothing (John 15:5). Nothing is a hard word to accept, but the reality is even our breath comes from God. Self-sufficiency hinders our reliance on God and damages our ability to enjoy friendships.

Self Rejection

Before he was anointed King, Saul was described as an impressive young man without equal (1 Sam 9:2). Even though he looked good, he struggled to accept himself – hiding among the baggage when he was proclaimed King (1Sam 10:20-23).

For many of us hiding among the baggage sounds like an easier option than facing a crowded room, or a conference alone. A modern equivalent of hiding in the baggage is looking at your phone!

The truth is you are fearfully and wonderfully made (Psalm 139:14). God has ordained for you every wonderful detail about your life (Psalm 139:16) and he rejoices over you with singing (Zeph 3:17)

What in your life hinders you from accepting who you are and developing friendships? Lack of money, physical appearance, clothes, past failure, jobs, speech, family or spouse? Take time to spend with God talking honestly with him about those areas you disqualify yourself in.

Self Pity

Saul was prone to a self pity party. Trouble with self-pity parties is no-one wants to come and no-one brings any presents.

The valiant commander of Israel made some petty accusations against those under him. *"all of you have conspired against me? No one discloses to me when my son makes a covenant with the son of Jesse. None of you is sorry for me or discloses to me that my son..." 1 Sam 22:8*

Self-pity is fed by suspicion and kills friendships because it is always questioning motives, words and actions.

If self-pity and suspicion is what you struggle with, meditate on 1 Cor 13:7 and allow the Lord to help you overcome self-pity and suspicion with His overflowing love.

Approval seeking

Saul blew it because he feared what the people thought of him (1 Sam 15:24). When we look for man's approval rather than enjoying the Father's approval won by Christ we are in trouble.

Some of the signs we are approval seeking are when we expect thanks for things we have done, when we want to keep up with the Jones, when we are disappointed friends don't commit on new clothes or hairstyle and when we behave differently when we know we are being watched.

Comparison

Saul kept "a jealous eye" on David, especially when the women started singing of how Saul killed thousands, but David tens of thousands. Theodore Roosevelt said that "Comparison is the thief of joy."

There will always be people better at things than us. Comparisons kill friendships. We compare our worst with our assumption of someone else's best. It can result in resentment towards others. The truth is we are the best at being us! Be happy with that!

Fear

Saul lived in fear – fear of the people (1 Sam 15:24), of Goliath (1 Sam 17:11) and the Philistine army (1 Sam 28:5)

Don't allow fear to dominate your life – fear of saying the wrong thing, people finding out about an area of our life, or having a disagreement.

We overcome fear by choosing not to let it control us and relying on God's perfect love to drive it out (1 John 4:18)

A better way

I was a lonely teenager. I struggled making friends and often fell out with people I wanted to be friends with. I remember facing up to some hard lessons in my early 20s and gradually becoming a more confident, gregarious extrovert. I went through Duncan Watkinson's book "True Friendship" with a friend and saw God change me powerfully through it.

The story of Jonathan and David's deep friendship shows us a better way. Jonathan was Saul's son and that shows us that we are not trapped by our genes or our upbringing. Saul was hopeless at friendship, his son Jonathan built a lasting friendship.

Deep Concern

Jonathan and David's hearts were knitted together (1 Sam 18:1). A deep concern for each other was evident.

Loyalty

They made a commitment to remain loyal to each other for ever. That's a "level 5" friendship that not many of us attain to, but it's a model for being more whole-heartedly committed to our friends.

Jonathan spoke well of David to Saul (1 Sam 19:4), when he heard of Saul's murderous intentions. Faithful friends praise in their absence and counter gossip, slander and loose talk.

Availability

They were available for each other and faithful. *"Whatever you say I will do for you." 1 Sam 20:4*

Encouragement

And Jonathan, Saul's son, rose and went to David at Horesh and strengthened his hand in God. 1 Sam 23:16

The greatness of their friendship meant that Jonathan helped David draw near to God at a low point.

The challenge is on to make friends that will stick closer than a brother and draw them to the Father – Friends, Food and the Gospel.

Application

1) Evaluate your friendships on the friendship scale – who do you know on the various levels?

2) What hindrances to friendship identified in the chapter do you need to take to the Lord

3) What friendships do you have that are anywhere near like David & Jonathan? How can they become more like it?

4) Plan to be friendly this week at all the levels of friendship.

6

Hospitality and Entertaining

Show hospitality to one another without grumbling. (1 Peter 4:9 ESV)

Rehabilitating Hospitality

Hospitality needs rehabilitating. If you mention the word in many churches, images of potluck fellowship suppers after a members' meeting come to mind. While good and probably fun, it is entirely missing the point and original meaning of the word hospitality.

The Biblical root of the word "Hospitality" is fascinating and similar. The Greek word is *Philoxenia* - which is two words joined together, The first is *philos* – which means kind affection or love and the second is *xenos*, which means stranger or foreigner. So the word hospitality, *Philoxenia*, means "one who loves strangers."

The English roots of hospitality are just as fascinating. In ancient times, religious leaders established international guest houses to look after pilgrims and travelling business. They were havens for guests, called hospices or hospitals from the Latin *hospes* – which means guest. By the time of the crusades these hospices, often run by monks, were the only safe places to stay. They then begun to specialize in looking after the poor, the sick and the injured, becoming what we now know as hospitals. By the 15th century the secular "hospitality" industry took over looking after travellers. Now the hospitality industry is a huge money maker. You can get a degree in it, while not practicing genuine hospitality at all.

Too often now our homes that were meant to be a haven for guests, have become a haven from guests. An Englishman's home is his castle is a massive British stronghold. A stronghold is a pattern of thinking often saturated in culture that hinders people from knowing God. In the 21st century, instead of drawing up the drawbridge and having a moat to protect us from unwanted visitors, curtains are drawn. We get home from a long day at work or school, or homemaking, lock the front door, pull the curtains and switch on the television or iPad. Home is where we get away from people. That kind of thinking is the opposite to Biblical hospitality – where your home is meant to be a hospital for the weary and a haven for the hurting.

The word hospitality, *Philoxenia*, means "one who loves strangers."

If we are going to make friends, eat good food together and see the gospel make an impact in our communities, we need to reverse that stronghold. I don't believe the right approach is to shout at the stronghold, or to pray against the spirit of castles! We tear down the British inhospitable mind-set by doing the Biblical opposite! So what is the Biblical opposite?

The idea of hospitality is not a potluck fellowship supper for church members, but loving and looking after strangers and foreigners so they get the chance to become part of the family. It is being willing and eager to welcome strangers and foreigners in with food and a bed, if needed, so they get a chance to become part of God's family.

Hospitality is a come and find us as we are kind of thing. It's a throw a couple of extra potatoes in the pan on a Sunday morning so you can invite some Church visitors back for lunch. It's a ring up some of the lonely and invite them round for a brew. When you have began to break the stronghold of inhospitality in your church, you'll find people will turn up unannounced and without making an appointment! That's a huge cultural issue for Brits and other cold climate cultures. The fear is that people will turn up when it is inconvenient, or when we are busy, the house is in a mess, or we have no food in. How do we handle that fear?

If someone turns up and it's really not convenient, say so and arrange another time. Think first, though, why is it inconvenient? Are you just wanting to watch the latest episode of a TV show that you could record? Are you embarrassed that the house is a mess? Or have you had people round three evenings this week and just need some time to recharge? If you are an introvert, you need time alone to recharge emotionally or you get drained. Block out some evenings for that. But do be open at other times to offer hospitality.

Jan and I do arrange to keep some free evenings in our diary, just not every single evening! Those "keep free" slots in the diary are inviolable without permission from both of us!

The word "Hospitality" occurs 10 times in the New Testament and give us a great insight into the genuine meaning of the word we have examined thus far. The top four instances are in Romans 12:13, 1 Timothy 3:1-6, 1 Peter 4:9 and Hebrew 13:1-2

Let's see what those verses can tell us...

1) Philadelphia Sandwiches

> *"Let brotherly love continue. Do not neglect to show hospitality to strangers, for thereby some have entertained angels unawares." Hebrews 13:1-2*

When most people talk about those verses the focus is often on the fact that you may show hospitality and find it was for an angel – just like Abraham did in Genesis 18.

The key thing in these two verses is actually the play on words between brotherly love and show hospitality, which we completely miss in English. Brotherly love is the Greek word "Philadelphia" – literally "love the brothers" and of course show hospitality is Philoxenia – love strangers. The author of Hebrews wants us to do both, to balance both – to love the brothers and love strangers and foreigners so they get to become brothers in Christ. Todd Adkins wrote "invite people to community before inviting them to conversion" on newchurches.com[vi]. It's a challenge to be like Levi (see chapter 7) – to mix our Christian and non-Christian friends together with food and trust the Spirit to be at work.

2) Don't grumble

1 Peter 4:9 exhorts us to

Show hospitality to one another without grumbling.

How often do you tell someone, "Pop by anytime" and then shudder when they do! Showing hospitality to people that just turn up is profoundly counter-cultural to the average Brit. In contrast I popped in at 1pm on some Africans in our church, having just already eaten my sandwiches, to find myself welcomed in and sat at table. A place was quickly set and there was plenty of food! They were ever ready culturally to show hospitality!

When we first moved to King's Lynn, Janet often invited school-gate mums back for coffee, but she never really had return invites. When she asked one of them why, the excuse was that they were about to have a new kitchen done. They were ashamed of their current kitchen and didn't want anyone around until it was all done. That's confusing entertaining with hospitality. Entertaining is a middle class pastime. It's inviting a few friends for a dinner party – best food, best china, trying to impress and hoping for an invite back. Hospitality is warts and all, come in, join us as we are and stay and be part of the family. The problem with entertaining, apart from that "comparison" attitude that sometimes goes with it, is the pressure it puts us under, the time it takes and how much it costs. Not many of us can entertain very often.

We have a fun TV show in the U.K. called "Come Dine with me" – one of our church planter friends in Helsinki was on it! The show puts four people against each other to entertain with a good meal. Contestants then vote on the quality of food, welcome and the winner gets £1,000. During the episode, fellow contestants have a "nosey" around the host's home looking for TV-friendly quirkiness or embarrassing things. That's "entertaining" at its worst! Hospitality is not a house inspection, it is friendship. No-one will remember how many lemony candles you had, but they will remember the friendship you showed, the laughs you had and the life-changing conversations that were had.

Here's a great quote from a widely shared blog I caught on Facebook recently:

Scruffy hospitality means you're not waiting for everything in your house to be in order before you host and serve friends in your home. Scruffy hospitality means you hunger more for good conversation and serving a simple meal of what you have, not what you don't have. Scruffy hospitality means you're more interested in quality conversation than the impression your home or lawn makes. If we only share meals with friends when we're excellent, we aren't truly sharing life together.

Don't allow a to-do list disqualify you from an evening with people you're called to love in friendship. Scheduling is hard enough in our world. If it's eating with kind, welcoming people in a less than perfect house versus eating alone, what do you think someone would choose? We tell our guests 'come as you are,' perhaps we should tell ourselves 'host as you are.[vii]

At the end of the post Father Jack challenges us

Go ahead and invite someone for tomorrow night. Keep your to-do list short. Take ten minutes to pick up the house and throw something together for dinner, even if it's from Trader Joe's. You're more ready than you think. And we're all hungry for genuine conversation more than we realize.[viii]

3) Hospitality is an eldership qualification

Most of the character qualifications of eldership in 1 Timothy 3:1-7 are just that, character qualifications. The questions asked show us if a prospective elder is someone worth following. Slipped in the list is "Hospitable." Being someone who welcomes strangers and foreigners in is a sign of Christian maturity. Elders set an example to follow and being hospitable requires elders to be outward looking and opening their homes to strangers and foreigners. It makes sure that elders of churches aren't just inwardly focused, they are outward looking.

4) Pursue Hospitality

Romans 12:13 is a similar exhortation to the one in Hebrews 13

"Contribute to the needs of the saints and seek to show hospitality."

Look after those within the church and seek or pursue loving strangers and foreigners by inviting them into your home so they get a chance to become part of the church family.

Hospitality is having that attitude of an open home, loving strangers and foreigners into the family. Again, keep it simple, keep it scruffy, but do it. In Bible times showing hospitality was something rich and poor did. When Jesus told the story of the persistent widow in Luke 18 asking for bread – it is because someone has turned up and she is showing hospitality but has nothing!

There is a place for the dinner party

For years I have taught on the difference between hospitality and entertaining to recover the Biblical practice of hospitality. It is a means of not only obeying Christ, but also showing love to those not yet part of God's family. And it makes it do-able by everyone.

As I prepared for a recent ten week sermon series on Meals with Jesus in Luke, I was shocked to find that dinner parties are also very much on God's agenda for Friends, Food and the Gospel. Of the ten meals in Luke, five are hospitality meals and five are dinner parties. Each one has a kingdom building, gospel spreading effect.

Passage	Which	Who	Outcome
5:27-39	Dinner Party	Levi mixes his Christian and non-Christian friends.	Kingdom of God is for all who repent.
7:36-50	Dinner party	Simon the Pharisee, gate-crashed by the sinful woman.	Repentance brings about reconciliation with people
9:10-17	Hospitality	Miraculous hospitality of bread and fish for 5,000.	The disciples take responsibility for an impossible miracle and rely on Jesus to provide.
10:38-42	Hospitality	At Mary and Martha's house.	Woman can be disciples. Prioritise God's presence first which empowers service.
11:37-54	Dinner party (luncheon)	Pharisees	Outward focused
14:1-24	Dinner party	Pharisee's house	Invite is for all – invite crippled, poor, lame and blind
19:1-10	Hospitality	At Zacchaeus' house	Jesus came to seek and save the lost
22:7-38	Dinner Party – in that it was pre-organised!	Passover/ Last Supper	Jesus performs the last Passover meal and initiates the Lord's supper
24:13-35	Hospitality	Cleopas's home after Emmaus road walk	Their eyes are opened as Jesus broke bread
24:36-53	Hospitality	With the 11 and others	You are witnesses!

It's important to lower the bar of having people round for a meal, so that people do it, without worrying about having to cook beyond their ability or means. Perhaps we have thrown the baby out with the bathwater though. Half those meals in Luke were dinner parties – more organised affairs, occasions to look forward to! The organized "dinner party" is a big part of "Friends, Food and the Gospel". The difference is in the attitude. We're not doing it to impress friends with how tidy the house is and how good we are at making elaborate food. We are maximizing friendship connections. We are providing opportunities for the Lord to be at work, as we mix Christians and not yet Christians together.

Supper parties, as my middle class friends call them, are a wonderful opportunity to mix Christians and non-Christians together with great food and thought given to who to invite and how to seat them!

We have defined hospitality properly from its origins to showing love to strangers and foreigners so they get to be part of the family. As I wrote "supper parties" in the last paragraph, it made me smile. In the UK the words we use for meals can be so confusing for people for whom English is a second or third language. Rest assured, they can be just as confusing for Brits too as they have regional meanings!

Here's my glossary of terms for *when we invite people round*, feel free to argue with me!

Tea – for adults, that's a cup of tea and a biscuit in the South East, with perhaps cakes and sandwiches in the more hospitable North and Northern Ireland. For children that will be a cooked meal! Within a family "tea" is usually the early evening cooked meal!

Afternoon tea – is cup of tea with scones (pronounced as in gone!), jam and cream. Which goes on first divides people from Devon and Cornwall quite well!

High Tea - is usually a cooked meal

Dinner – that's an invite to a full evening meal, possibly with other guests.

Dinner Party – that's an invite to a full evening meal, that carries a sense of occasion like a birthday. Dress up and bring a bottle!

Supper - for the middle classes in the South East, that's also an invite to a full evening meal. Elsewhere it may be an invite for a later on after event snack with you.

Whatever term you use for an invited meal, be clear what it is, be hospitable and mix non-Christians and Christians together. You can do simple hospitality or more formal parties for the Gospel just like Levi in the next chapter.

Application

1 What has held you back from hospitality and why?

2 When was the last time you offered Biblical hospitality?

3 When was the last time you mixed some Christian and non-Christian friends for a dinner party?

4 Invite some people for a meal tomorrow, keep it simple, but do it!

7

Levi's example

Ana Levi made him a great feast in his house, ana there was a large company oj tax collectors ana others reclining at table with them. (Luke 5:29 ESV)

The story of Levi in Luke 5:27-32 is a fantastic example of Friends, Food and the Gospel and a dinner party.

After this he went out and saw a tax collector named Levi, sitting at the tax booth. And he said to him, "Follow me." And leaving everything, he rose and followed him.

And Levi made him a great feast in his house, and there was a large company of tax collectors and others reclining at table with them. And the Pharisees and their scribes grumbled at his disciples, saying, "Why do you eat and drink with tax collectors and sinners?" And Jesus answered them, "Those who are well have no need of a physician, but those who are sick. I have not come to call the righteous but sinners to repentance." (Luke 5:27-32 ESV)

Levi's Background

Levi was a tax collector by profession. Tax was as big an issue then as it is now. And there was just as much corruption around it too.

Today we have the problem of the rich and the establishment avoiding paying their fair share of tax, so education and hospitals suffer. As I write this Presidential hopeful Donal Trump has just boasted of not paying Federal taxes for 20 years. Then they had the problem that too much was collected and filled the pockets of the rich. Actually that's the same problem!

There were two types of tax in the Roman Empire 2000 years ago. The "Gabbai" was a general tax on property and income and the "Mokkhe" functioned like a customs tax of 2-5% on goods. Although the Roman occupiers got the taxes, they had long ago learned that Roman tax collectors would be murdered by Jewish zealots. So they sold tax collecting franchises to Jews - because no Jewish zealot would murder a Jew, even an evil collaborating one.

> He is now going to be "God's go-between."

Great Mokkhe's, like Zacchaeus would buy a franchise then employ Little Mokkhe's to set up booths wherever they could to rip people off as they passed with goods to and from market. As you took goods on the way to market you could be stopped by a little Mokkhe to pay tax on your produce and then again on the way back to be taxed again with what you had bought or your income from selling the produce.

Levi is a Little Mokkhe in his tax booth, who possibly had employed thugs to force people to stop and pay tax on whatever they had in their possession. He would not have been a popular person and won't have had many friends outside the profession.

His name Levi means he is from the tribe of Levi, a Levite, the tribe from where God called priests. They were meant to be "God's go-betweens." Names were important then and were often picked prophetically for their meaning. Perhaps his parents hoped he'd grow up to be a priest, God's go-between. But sin had made him the opposite of his destiny. He has become a "Rome's go-between."

Some scholars think he may have set up his booth on the road deliberately at the edge of the crowds that were following Jesus, to get more money, little knowing He is about to have his life transformed by an encounter with Jesus.

His parents had named him prophetically, hoping he would become a priest. But sin and greed had messed him up and he was missing his destiny. In the way that God does, Levi is ambushed by Jesus and put back on his destiny - He is now going to be "God's go-between." His life is back on its prophetic destiny - he's following Jesus and will be a fisher of men! God holds your destiny - you may have been missing it, but God can sort it out. It's never too late to get on the right path! God is good!

Levi's Dinner Party

The first thing Levi does is to hold a great feast. He's the first to grasp Friends, Food and the Gospel.

A "great feast" was called a symposium in ancient times (now that means a particularly boring conference), but back then it was a middle class banquet. It would have been a fairly formal dinner party, with a planned guest list and special invites. Guests reclined on couches around a table. It would start with a banquet for the men and then move onto the *sumposium* which often meant a drinking party, but one where the conversation was steered by the guest of honour around a topic.

In contrast, the hospitality meal was the one where anyone and everyone - rich or poor would open their homes for people to be fed and often put up for the night. Jesus and then his followers radically turn both the feast and hospitality meal upside down. He breaks convention, because everyone men, women, slaves and even Samaritans are welcome. And there is no drunken debauchery!

Levi, or Matthew has organised a great feast - a planned party - he wants his non believing friends to meet the guest of honour Jesus and his new Christian friends.

His non-believing friends were a bunch of tax collectors - first century tax collectors. So imagine the conversation – the best ways of extortion, who provides the best thugs, the skin trade and who is the best at loan sharking. Mix in Jesus, the disciples and the Holy Spirit in the midst doing His thing.

No-one is too far away to be a recipient of the love of Christ. And here we have a story of Jesus hanging out with sinners to draw them to a changed life - to repentance.

The kingdom of God is a party and Christ invites us to a great party - a celebration of grace - getting the undeserved favour of God to be forgiven and changed and accepted and loved, even if you are a traitor, a thug, the lowest of the low or a rich exploiter of the poor.

And this is how Janet and I have chosen to live life. This is an expression for us of having generous hearts - throwing parties where we get our non-Christian and Christian friends together and trusting that the Holy Spirit will be at work. And He is - most of the conversions to Christ in our church have started at a party.

Some of our small groups can throw a great feast, a symposium and other groups the simple hospitality meal, Jesus used both to reach lost people – rich and poor. It really doesn't matter how grand. In fact we often do jackets and bring a filling – simple and cheap. It's about people, not the menu!

The Pharisees reaction

In Luke 5v30 the Pharisees are grumbling and religious people love to grumble, because it comes from pride.

"Why is Jesus going to one of those parties?" they ask. The hypocrisy is astounding, because they were there too - v29 the Pharisees were part of the others that were there. They were grumbling at Jesus being there, not looking down on the sinners but helping them, forgiving them, saving them. Levi had already left his old life and had begun to follow Jesus, leaving everything behind. The new him was radically different from the old him. And he had hosted a great feast with Jesus and his new friends and some of the religious Pharisees AND his old friends.

The Pharisees were ready to be with Jesus and the disciples at this early stage of His ministry on earth, but objected to the unrighteous being there.

Jesus' reply is great! He uses analogy, Scripture and personal authority.

i)   **Analogy.** Doctors are for sick people. You don't make a doctor's appointment when you are completely healthy to tell them how healthy you are. You go when there is something wrong and you need fixing. Why couldn't they see how important it was for Jesus to go to feasts like this where there are sinners who need saving?

ii)   **Scripture.** In Matthew's own account 9:13 Jesus says *"Go and learn what this means."* Ouch, that is pretty cutting! Quoting "I desire mercy and not sacrifice" from

Hosea 6:6. He's telling the Scripture experts to go and learn what Scripture means!

iii)   **Personal authority.** The Pharisees who were at the banquet are being told they are sin sick too. They were there, Jesus was there. He's the great Physician who heals the sin sick. So the implication is they are just as sinful as the people they call sinners. There's a healthy dose of irony and sarcasm there.

Levi's example teaches us the value of mixing non-Christian and Christian friends together in social settings so we end up with Friends, Food and the Gospel.

Religious people didn't like what Levi was doing. They were hypocrites! The Pharisees were clearly there and probably indulging in what they were criticising. They certainly didn't like the way Jesus uses friends, food and the Gospel as a means of grace for people to find Jesus.

Application

1 Levi had been "Rome's go-between" and now was living in his true identity as "God's go-between". What is your identity in Christ?

2 How are your non-Christian friends? If you don't have any, what will you do to make some?

3 If your small group will apply this book, when and what will be the next feast?

4 If you don't have small groups in your church setting, how will you gather a fishing team?

8

Friends, Food and the Gospel in practice

What you have learned and received and heard and seen in me—practice these things, and the God of peace will be with you. (Philippians 4:9 ESV)

So far we have identified the kingdom of God is a feast, worked out your evangelistic style, so you can work in a team to fish, and seen that making disciples is a process. We have learnt some principles for building friendships. We have seen the Biblical call to be hospitable and how Jesus used simple hospitality and dinner parties to make His Good News known. Now we can get to the meat!

There are lots of ways that we can team fish. If you all have common interests like football, walking, badminton or playing bridge, you can join a club and make new friends together. A few years ago Janet and I took up jogging, to counteract the effects of so many pizza parties! We started doing the local Parkrun (a weekly timed 5k run in local parks all over the UK and beyond), meeting lots of new friends and progressed from there to the local running club. We have already been able to connect other runners into our small group community and one just came to a guest service a fortnight ago.

When it comes to team fishing, anything goes that is not sinful. We are looking to do activities together where people can talk while they are doing what they are doing. That's why going to the cinema is a terrible activity for building friendships, unless you do something after the film together!

> We are always looking for excuses to throw a party

Each of those activities are only liked by some people, so not everyone can or will want to get involved or will be reached. There is one thing that we all do however, one thing that we all have in common. That is eating food. There are not many cultures where it is unacceptable to eat with others. It is the one of the most powerful ways we show friendship and enjoy each other's company.

Earlier I showed you the journey that most people go on to become a disciple. They start out not knowing any Christians, then they become open to friendship as they start to meet your small group. Gradually they open up to the message. Then one day they are ready, ready to commit to following Jesus and becoming a disciple. In the same way individuals go on a journey towards discipleship, there's a journey in friendship and food! I have to got to admit I'm struggling as I write this chapter as what we do is relaxed and naturally supernatural. In writing it down, it's going to sound like a formula. So do please think of it as a natural process rather than a rigid formula!

Start Small

We were recently invited for supper at a church family's home. We'd never been before and I found myself nervous at who else would be there. The funny thing is that I am an extrovert, at my happiest meeting new people. And yet I was nervous. Who would be there? What will we talk about? We ended up having a super evening, meeting some new people and having a lot of fun over some delicious food.

Sometime we make it hard for people to come to things. Our friend is being invited to a big social, with lots of people there they don't know. They are not sure what to expect and for a lot of people that is just too big a barrier, so they politely decline.

So we encourage our group to mix non-Christians and Christians in **small settings first**, in twos and threes. Go out for coffee, have a couple of people for a BBQ or supper. Then as non-Christian friends get to know other Christians in the group it is easier for them to come to a larger scale social because they know some people already. If that sounds like you have to add extra activities to your already busy life, you don't. I just do what I normally do, with people, always thinking what non-Christians can I mix with Christians as I do it? I love the fact that one of our small group posted pictures on Facebook of a fence painting party – where lots of people came to help paint someone's long fence. That's community and they seemed to enjoy it. I am hoping that they ate together afterwards, instead of watching the paint dry!

Any excuse to party

As the community of the group begins to grow with Christians and non-Christians getting together in smaller groups, we begin to add bigger parties to the mix. Remember that it is as a non-Christian gets to know a whole group of Christians they begin to really see the difference that Jesus makes to us. They have begun to hear the stories from the storytellers, have had questions answered by Reasoners, had the secrets of the heart impacted by Power Style people and begun to be confronted with the good news of the Gospel by Harvesters, while being served great food by the Servants!

When it comes to bigger socials, we are always looking for excuses to throw a food party – national and international holidays, birthdays, a sunny day (they are fairly rare in the UK), a baptism. Whenever we can!

National theme nights work really well. Often someone from a nation will show us how to make their national dish. We have learnt how to make sushi, spring rolls and had an Italian teach us how to make pasta and served up the 2.5kg of Fettuccine we made to 25 people. A Mexican student made us all Tacos. We've done curry nights where everyone brings a different curry. International food evenings, where everyone brings a dish from their nation (or nation they wish they were from!).

Other types of theme nights are where we celebrate a national holiday. On St Patricks Day in March, everyone seems to be Irish, so brings Irish dishes or green food!

At the end of January we celebrate Burns night, where we put on a traditional Scottish Burns night with haggis, neaps and tatties, a toast to the haggis and to the Lassies (Ladies). We have even celebrated international Pi day with a bring a pie evening. I'll admit that was the most tenuous excuse we've had.

We've been doing this so long and posting so many photos on Facebook, that people really want to come to our parties! Facebook is a great tool for Friends, Food and the Gospel. We make an album of anything we do, fill it with photos and tag everyone. People are nosey, they click on friends photos to see who is who and what is what. The best way to treat Facebook is only post things you don't mind the whole world knowing and leave the settings open. (Bit like not casting your pearls before swine!)

Keeping Momentum

Our normal small group evenings are a chance to get together weekly to worship, discuss and apply the sermon and minister to one another. To keep momentum for being outward looking with Friends, Food and the Gospel, we always give ten minutes at the end to pray for friends and plan the next social. As soon as one food social is completed we start planning the next, averaging one every 4-6 weeks.

Envisioning the Small Group

Friends, Food and the Gospel really took over when we were able to envision the group in the concept of their style of evangelism and working as a team together. I remember a memorable evening after the first pizza party that had gone really well. Janet and I encouraged each member of the group as to how they had served, connected, jammed on a guitar to help make the evening go well. It was at that moment they grasped team work makes the dream work! It wasn't long after we all saw the first harvest from what we had been doing.

We are completely passionate about Friends, Food and the Gospel and constantly share the vision with the group. I'm writing this at the end of a summer break where we have said goodbye to dear friends who have been impacted by the Gospel through our small group. Friends that have become Christians, been filled with the Spirit, gone from lukewarm followers to passionate disciples and have now moved on to their next medical placement as junior doctors or back to their home countries. Already we are getting ready for the next wave to begin to come through – friends that were brought by those who have gone, running club buddies who have been attracted by Facebook photos of parties and new school language assistants and junior doctors who are being grabbed as I write by Connectors in the group.

People continually say to Janet, how can you do it, working as a teacher and having a family? Her answer is that it is not a chore if you are passionate about it! That said we do make sure we have time to recover after each big party.

Passion is important in leadership – it inspires followers. We keep sharing the vision and encouraging, especially as some people move on before grasping the grace of God and others never seem to go from Open to friendship to Open to the Message.

Our experience is that small groups that are lead by connectors will be best placed to put Friends, Food and the Gospel into practice. When I am looking for small group leaders, I am looking for a heart for God as well as for people. Would I look forward to meeting them for a coffee or a pint?

K.I.S.S.

If that sounds hard to do, we actually keep it as simple as possible. All our food evenings are bring and share – so everyone is asked to bring a big bowl of something or drinks. Those that are more "Can't cook, won't cook" bring drinks or nibbles and we make sure that it is accessible for everyone.

One of the best starter food evenings, certainly in the UK context, is bring a jacket potato filling. A jacket potato is a potato baked in its' skin. They just need cleaning, pricking (so they don't burst), wiping with olive oil and baking in an oven for a few hours at 180oC. Everyone brings a filling – some grated cheese, coleslaw, a chilli, a curry or whatever and we enjoy it together!

We have learned to be very specific when getting people to bring food. Language barriers can sometimes be an obstacle. At a recent event, we asked one of our Spanish nurses to bring a pudding. Thankfully we clarified what "pudding" means as she thought that meant a salad!

We also encourage people to be generous, telling them in advance how many are expected. We don't expect first-timers to bring anything unless they ask to. Once part of the community, then they can muck in too!

It is worth investing in lots of cheap plates and cutlery – as paper plates don't really work resting on knees in a packed out living room or garden.

On the cultural and international evenings, someone may bring some traditional music, or a quiz or teach us how to cook the food.

The Connectors bring friends, the Servants cook or help serve and clear up and the Reasoners, Storytellers, Power types and Harvesters await opportunities to share and promptings from the Spirit. All while lots of eating, fun, laughter and occasionally dancing is happening.

Pizza!

The parties we like doing most are pizza parties. We now have a brick pizza oven in our garden, made for us by a local builder (www.buildyourownpizzaoven.com). We fire it up in the afternoon, so the inside is around 400oC and then cook simple thin crust Napoli pizzas – which take 90seconds to cook. People love having a go at stretching dough, or putting toppings on or cooking them in the oven. Pizza is simple to make and a very cheap way to feed lots of people – the cheese is the most expensive ingredient.

We will then light up a fire pit and sit around eating pizza until our bellies ache. Then a guitar will appear and songs are sung while marshmallows are roasted and people chat.

I have lots of stories of journeys of faith that started at these evenings. Two Chinese students became Christians through the bridge to life diagram on the back of an envelope after a St Patricks night. An Italian came to faith not long after teaching us all how to make pasta. A young Mexican lady, from a Catholic background, was filled with the Spirit not long after the Taco evening. Food evenings are a brilliant way of building an international church. Food transcends and bridges cultures.

Whole Church Socials

We also do very larger scale food socials. We have an annual international food evening in a hall, where everyone brings a dish from his or her nation and there is cultural entertainment.

We have an annual barn dance and hog roast and more frequently we do bring and share lunches after Sunday gatherings. For safety we ask people to bring a serving utensil for their dish and mark it up with allergens like nuts, which may mean it needs to be on a separate table.

The Alpha Course is becoming for us a fantastic tool for reaping and beginning discipleship. We recently did it as a small group as a finale to the academic year. After a year or so of food evenings and pizza parties, Alpha was a natural and very fruitful next step.

If you are a process kind of person, here's what we do…

The process

i)   Ones and twos meet up with friends

ii) Small group food events – Guy Fawkes night, Christmas dinner, Burns Night, St Patricks' Night, International themed nights

iii) Alpha / Christianity Unwrapped.

Repeat!

Friends, Food and the Gospel. In essence we make friends and work as a team to expose them to our loving community through as many food parties as we can trusting the Holy Spirit to work as we bring Christians and non-Christians together.

Application

1 What food evenings could your group put on?

2 In your small group, begin to plan your next party!

3 How will you work together as a team to put it on - using everyone's gifts and evangelism styles?

4 If you are a small group leader, how will you ensure each person in your group gets caught up in the vision?

9

Loving the foreigner

Then she fell on her face, bowing to the ground, ana saia to him, "Why have I founa favour in your eyes, that you shoula take notice oj me, since I am a foreigner?' (Ruth 2:10 ESV)

One of the biggest mistakes of the Church Growth Movement is the "homogenous unit principle." This is the idea that churches grow when you target a particular demographic group. They can and do grow faster, but it is certainly not what God has in mind for His glorious church. Many of the problems of racism in the USA and the problems we will experience as Brexit takes effect, will be solved by churches that are intentionally one new man in Christ. The people of God is meant to be made up of every tribe and tongue. Not just White middle class people, or Africans or Skateboarders or whatever people group you feel called to. The church is made up of all tribes, tongues, ages and classes. The miracle of the Gospel is that it reconciles people to God and to each other and brings them into the God's family.

Abraham was called by God to be the Father of Israel, the Old Testament people of God in Gen 12. God told him

> *"And I will make you into a great nation and I will bless you and make your name great, so that you will be a blessing. I will bless those who bless you and him who dishonours you I will curse and in you all the families of the earth will be blessed."*

God's call on Abraham was to be a blessing to the nations. Centuries later, Moses was called to rescue Israel from slavery and Egypt. When they reached Mount Sinai, The Lord reframed the original call to bless the nations with these words

"You shall be my treasured possession among all the people, for all the earth is mine and you shall be to me a kingdom of priests and a holy nation." Exodus 19:5-6

They are God's treasured possession first and foremost. Their identity is deeply rooted in their relationship with God. They are then called to balance being priests – mediating God to others and being holy – set apart in holiness. Sadly they treated that more as a pendulum than a balanced lifestyle. The pendulum often swung to being so caught up with the people they were meant to be mediating God too, they took on sinful practices and made them worse. Then at other times, they separated themselves completely in "holiness", calling Gentiles dogs. They just could never do it.

Peter repeats the call in 1 Peter 2:9. The difference now is that we have the Holy Spirit empowering us to do it! It's interesting to see that when the Spirit came at Pentecost, He came and reversed the curse of Babel – not understanding each other's languages and gave tongues and interpretation, so that the peoples from the nations around Israel could hear the wonders of the Gospel in their own languages.

The early church took a while to get it though. They stayed in Jerusalem reaching Jews for Jesus for years, before persecution scattered them to Judea, Samaria and the ends of the earth. It took a vision for Peter to grasp the gospel is for Gentiles too. And no-one would lay their hands on Cornelius to impart the Spirit, so the Spirit did it sovereignly!

The early church did get it and began to see the gospel spread to all nations, obeying Christ's great commission to make disciples of all people groups!

One day there will be a feast, when Jesus returns and there will be multitudes "from every tribe and language and people and nations." Rev 5:9-10. I want earth to be as much like heaven as possible so I am committed to planting churches that are thoroughly multi-national.

Friends, food and the gospel works so well in multi-national churches. Food and the gospel are two things that bring people from different backgrounds together.

> Any church can be multi-cultural anywhere, not just in large cities where many nations are gathered.

It was such a privilege to meet and visit Markus and Ellen Adolfsson. They lead a marvellously multi-cultural church in a small village in the centre of Sweden. They embody and show that any church can be multi-cultural anywhere, not just in large cities where many nations are gathered. They introduced us to international food evenings as a way of gathering peoples together to enjoy each other's food and show off cultural entertainment. Language barriers are no longer a barrier when you are eating and dancing!

We are working and living in King's Lynn which is a 97.3% white market town in the East of England (with a large number of white Eastern European migrants.) Our church has had 30 different nations as part of our community – with at least 20 nations gathered every Sunday. People say we must be a multi-cultural town. I answer no it's not, but we love the nations, and the nations gather around the gospel!

How do we love the foreigner? Multi-ethnic vs Multi-cultural

Lots of churches gather people from different ethnic backgrounds, but they are still mono-cultural in that everyone listens to the same music, eats the same food and goes to the same entertainment. That's multi-ethnic rather than multi-cultural. Being multi-cultural involves us intentionally engaging different cultures and embracing differences and similarities.

It slows down ministry because genuine multi-cultural friendships and relationships require transparency and trust that takes time to build. Slow food is better than fast food and real brewed coffee is better than instant coffee. Multi-cultural ministry is slow brewed but better and what God tells us the new heaven on earth will be like!

It's a recipe for conflict. There will be hurt feelings and cross-cultural gaffes a plenty. My most embarrassing story is when I tried to introduce myself in German on a Sunday morning when we had 50 German students visiting. I wanted to tell them I was the leader of the church, so I said "Ich bin der führer des Gateway Church." I didn't get to finish the sentence, as there was a loud gasp of horror about halfway through. Afterwards, one of the young people told me it was the absolute technically correct word for leader, but not used anymore!

Multi-cultural friendships are a recipe for conflict because of cross-cultural misunderstandings. Cultures handle conflict very differently. My Dutch fellow elder is very direct and came up to me after a sermon to tell me "You spoke too fast today, the EAL (English as an Additional Language) people wouldn't have understood you. Slow down!" He then paused and told me, "But it was good! Slow down." The Dutch say it how it is without flowers! The Brits are more reserved, but will say it eventually.

With cross-cultural friendships, there will be issues and conflict that are exacerbated by how different cultures. We recently had a delightful Nigerian lady turn up who had a very English name. Within two minutes she was telling us that Nigerians with English names are descended from slaves who had been deported to the USA/UK and then they or descendants had made it back. The fact that all came out within minutes shows the pain cultures have experienced at the hands of other cultures can be raw for centuries.

Cross cultural means linguistic misunderstandings

Even within one language, words are used differently. My children insist that something that is good is sick! I still struggle with good things being wicked!

Overleaf is a chart floating around social media that illustrates cross-cultural misunderstanding perfectly.

What the British say	What the British mean.	What others understood
I hear what you say.	I disagree and don't want to discuss it further.	He accepts my point of view.
That's not bad.	That's good.	That's poor.
Oh, incidentally/by the way…	The primary purpose this conversation is…	That is not very important
You must come for dinner.	It's not an invitation, I am just being polite.	I will get an invitation soon.

Handling conflict in multi-cultural settings

Transparency and trust are built when you recognise how cultures handle conflict – directly, indirectly and work through well.

When an Asian fell out with a Brit recently, culturally they wouldn't approach the person directly with the issue, but dropped a hint to a third party about the issue. The hint to action was missed and the issue therefore stewed, until it blew up. Dealing with cross cultural conflict and issues often means unravelling the cultural before the issue itself.

Timekeeping

Another major issue is time – Western cultures value time-keeping and appointments. Warmer climate cultures value relationship over time management – so if they meet someone on the way they will stop and visit rather than look at their watch and hurry on.

Cultural values are different, not necessarily better or worse! Or right or wrong. When building cross-cultural relationships, we need to seek to understand cultural values rather than criticise them.

Janet & I were invited for a meal by some Sri-Lankans. When we arrived there were only two places set at the table. We sat and food was brought out and we ate while the family watched. They would eat when we left. That felt really awkward to us who normally share food together. How much do we eat? How much do we leave? Why are they watching us quietly? To them, they were showing us very great honour by serving us first and eating what was left.

Asking questions to understand cultures is so important. But so is listening. It's easy to spot unique things about other cultures than it is your own. An Indian family asked us why we don't do all age small groups and have them on a Friday so it is not a school night. Then they said. "Oh that's because it's your family night." I'd never realised that UK churches don't organise much on a Friday, because that's... er... our family night!

Given cross-cultural challenges, we have still found that a Friends, Food and the Gospel strategy for growing the church with new disciples is fantastic for growing a genuinely multi-cultural church.

Pretty much all of our food parties have an international flavour and an emphasis of understanding one another's cultures which has been a great way to build a multi-cultural church.

Refugees and Asylum Seekers

As the humanitarian crisis grows in Syria, Iraq and Afghanistan, millions of refugees have begun the terrifying and dangerous journey to safer countries. We have to remember that 2000 years ago a young poor family made a similar journey from Bethlehem to Egypt.

The reaction in many European nations has been one of fear and ghettoization. I'm appalled how few refugees the U.K. agreed to take over five years. But there has been really encouraging signs of hospitality amongst the churches within the family of churches I am part of in Relational Mission.

Refugee ministry in the Netherlands

Jonathan and Nolda Tipping have excelled at hosting parties for refugees in their large garden in Onnen, Netherlands.

Here is their story. Jonathan and I were wondering what our calling was at the place where we lived and worked. We wanted to be more of a witness, be more missional. In this period a refugee centre opened less than 1 km from our house. We did not have to go to the nations but the nations were coming to us. The centre houses families mainly from Syria and Eritrea, both countries in the grips of evil regimes of terror and abuse. The 500 refugees in the centre almost double the size of our quiet rural village.

The next question we asked was how do we as local Christians serve and show love to our new neighbours. We initially sent a request out to the church and friends for gifts of clothes, buggies and bikes (in the Netherlands it is difficult to function without a bike!). The response was overwhelming. It took four or five fully loaded cars to bring everything to the centre where we added the donations to the growing mountain of clothes. The staff at the centre eventually had to call a halt to the stream of gifts. They did not have enough staff to process and hand everything out. This initial effort was a good initiative.

We were not that satisfied with the outcome as seemed to be very impersonal and did not bring us into contact with the refugees. We wanted to find ways in which we, as a Christian community, could meet and serve our new neighbours. We had heard of a Dutch Christian charity that helped Christians throughout the Netherlands establish links with refugee centres. We contacted them and they agreed to come to give an introduction to the issue. An invitation was sent out to local churches of all the various denominations to find volunteers for this work. We opened up our house, expecting only a dozen or so people to turn up. In fact around sixty people attended and we were forced to hold our meeting in the garden. Thankfully we were blessed with good weather. It was so amazing to see Christians build bridges over denominational differences for the sake of the Gospel.

An outcome of this meeting was the establishment of a network for refugees (simplified in Dutch to the organisation's name 'Vlechtwerk'). The primary aim of this network is to encourage and facilitate the building of relationships between the refugees and local residents (especially Christians). Jonathan and I work in a coordinating team to help link the giftings of volunteers with the needs of the refugees. It has been amazing to see that, amongst the busyness of our everyday family, work, church and social life, God gives us the energy and opportunity for this. Although the group did not want to focus on activities, we decided to kick-start the initiative with a 'getting to know each other' party in our garden. We wanted the party to be as informal and relaxed as possible and we knew from experience that asking guests to bring their own food and all share this together is a great way to facilitate this.

The initial plans were for a relatively small, intimate gathering. However we had the feeling we should be prepared for something bigger. The amazing thing was that the more we needed to organise, the more volunteers came forward to assist us. A Syrian Christian translated the flyer into Arabic. My brother and his wife sent a press release to the local press agencies. Ladies from our missional community took responsibility to decorate the party tent. Syrian refugees and men from the neighbourhood worked together to set up the tents. We even had a farmer deliver chairs from a nearby church using the scoop of his tractor. It was great to see so many people working together, using their talents and own resources.

The day of the refugee party came. We had no idea what to expect but were confident God would work everything out. Although it was October we had fabulous clear, sunny weather which meant we could use the outdoor space and not have to all cram into the tent. We had a slow trickle of visitors at the start, mainly Dutch volunteers from the area. However, putting up Arabic signs on the street and canvassing the refugee centre helped to attract the crowds. Soon it was difficult to keep track of who was coming and going.

We estimated afterwards that we must have had at least three hundred guests, two thirds of whom were refugees. It was an incredible atmosphere with people from all different cultures mixing and sharing stories. Many children also showed up and thoroughly enjoyed playing sports in the garden or doing crafts in the studio. It was also nice to see a few elderly refugees sit on the fringes of the crowd simply enjoying watching all that was going on.

At some point, one of the Syrian guys managed to plug his phone into the PA system to play a few Middle Eastern tunes. It didn't take long for a group of men to start singing and dancing. This spurred on the Eritrean guys to do the same. You could see that these simple acts made everyone feel more at home and create a rest-bite from the troubles they have had to endure. In the same way as sharing food, we could see how music and dance relaxes people and gives opportunities for cross-cultural friendships to grow.

One of my favourite moments was when I was introduced to a group of Syrian ladies who had meticulously prepared traditional dishes to share with everyone. This included a plate of baklava, a sweet pastry made in the Turkish-Syrian region. It was no surprise that within minutes this dessert disappeared. The ladies were so proud that they were able to contribute. You could see that in some way it restored their dignity.

> Yesterday was so much fun! When can we do it again?

Various people from local media organisations turned up to the party. This included a man from the local television station who came to film the event and record interviews with the guests. He had worked for some years as a correspondent in Eritrea so this assignment really interested him. In fact, after he had finished recording his broadcast, he packed his camera away in his van and returned to enjoy the festivities. His news report the following day was highly positive, which was in stark contrast to the negative press that filled the airwaves about the Dutch refugee crisis. The news item of our party was posted on Facebook and within days got over a quarter of a million views. People in the Netherlands were hungry for a real and uplifting news item about the immigration situation.

We have seen that cross cultural events like this combined with social media can help to sow a seed for the Gospel. Months after the event, we are still getting comments from people about what a wonderful idea it was to organize something for the refugees. This gives us an opportunity so say that it was not just us, but a whole group of local Christians who did something.

We asked volunteers during the party to exchange phone numbers with asylum seekers and then stay in touch with them. We have been really encouraged to hear that many people have started friendships and are regularly meeting up. During the party, we did not have that much time to spend with our own three children and this is something I felt quite guilty about. However the following day at breakfast they all were shouting "Yesterday was so much fun! When can we do it again?" Jonathan and I still remember this as one of the most memorable days of our lives. It was like having a bit of heaven on earth and experiencing God in an almost tangible way. Since the first one we have had various smaller BBQ parties at our house where we invite both refugees, neighbours and people from church. For all three groups these BBQs are often life changing and unforgettable. We have given a similar big party in May 2016 (250 people) and are planning for a 300+ party in September.

We feel that these gatherings, both big and small have transformed our view of Gods kingdom here on earth and we see transformation with everyone who volunteered. We are still in touch with quite a few refugees that we got to know at this party and we notice too that this party has created openings. We have since built further relationships through organizing Dutch lessons, sports events and games nights. We have also recently arranged for a group of young refugees to visit the university to meet students and see how the Dutch education system works.

Being hospitable and creating bridges between groups in society is as much giving as receiving. It is a tangible way of seeing Gods kingdom being established in our own neighbourhood.

Looking after refugees in Southern Germany

The Evangelische Freikirche Steinen led by my friend Gerhard Pfeander responded magnificently to the influx of refugees in their small town. Here is Gerhard's story.

In September 2015 our local authorities announced that at the end of September our town would get about 100 refugees in tents on the lawn of our outdoor public swimming pool for six weeks.

So our church of 120 members asked ourselves: "What can we do to serve these refugees?" In Germany it can be quite cold and wet in October/November, so we had the idea to open our church centre every afternoon from Monday to Friday for three hours. Our local authorities invited any interested parties to a meeting. We announced this idea to them. The council even asked if we could have the "Room for clothes" in our church centre where the refugees could get clothes for free. We were happy to say "yes" and so the refugees could come to our church centre to get clothes, coffee, tea and cakes in a warm and dry room. They could also play table tennis or table football and could use our kitchen to cook their own food (which the Africans especially liked to do). We had days when nearly all the refugees came to our place and the least that came was about twenty.

Every day, one person from our church was responsible for the afternoon and was helped by 5-7 people from our church and other churches in our town. We had refugees from Gambia, Syria, Albania and Macedonia.

Some were eager to learn German, so we ran lessons and even used a children's bible to teach them German. Also we had Bibles from all of the languages of the refugees and were able to distribute these to them.

One afternoon I met a young man from Gambia at the door, greeted him and we began to talk to each other. Suddenly I realized that his iPhone was on and somebody was speaking. I apologized for interrupting him but he said: "I am only listening to the preaching of an imam..." and put it off. A few minutes later he was sitting at a table, drinking coffee and reading a children bible with one of our helpers.

A young woman from our church, who is Turkish, but grew up in Germany, found out that two young Syrian women spoke Turkish – they had learned it in a refugee camp in Turkey where they had to stay for two years. Both sides were surprised that they could speak to each other and our Turkish lady could share with them how she became a Christian and proclaim the Gospel to them.

After six weeks, at the beginning of November, the refugees had to leave the tents and moved to an empty factory in another town!

We were lucky to be able to serve them for six weeks and are sure that God will save some of them!

Application

1) How many nationalities are you involved with?

2) What issues have you had to face and work through cross-cultural in your setting?

3) What can your church do to help love the foreigner better?

10

Helping people cross the line of faith

Now when they heard this they were cut to the heart, and said to Peter and the rest of the apostles, "Brothers, what shall we do?" And Peter said to them, "Repent and be baptized every one of you in the name of Jesus Christ for the forgiveness of your sins, and you will receive the gift of the Holy Spirit. (Acts 2:37-38 ESV)

The Gospel

The gospel is incredible. The good news of Jesus Christ reconciling us to the Father is breath-taking. Our broken relationship with God due to our sin is dealt with at the cross, so we can enjoy fellowship and blessing of knowing God the Father, Son and Spirit.

If like me you have undergone evangelism training, you will have been taught methods of sharing the gospel that deal with our guilt. The Navigators "Bridge to Life"™, Campus Crusade's "Four Spiritual Laws", or the Roman Road. These are all fantastic tools for helping us to lead people to cross the line of faith and become a disciple. My favourite is the Bridge to Life and I have lost count of the times I have used it on the back of an envelope or serviette, to lead people to the Saviour.

As we have reached out to friends from different cultures we have discovered that we have a very Western concept of our need for the Gospel – based on innocence/guilt. Our Western worldview means we wear western spectacles when we read the Scriptures. Westerners understand their need of saving grace as guilt. When the Holy Spirit convicts, it will be largely guilt that we feel. We love the book of Romans considering it the summit of the New Testament for its presentation of the gospel of grace setting us free from the Law and justifying us by faith. Justification means we are declared not only not guilty, but righteous by putting our faith in Jesus. As a westerner, I see the Bible primarily dealing with God's law, guilt and grace. Interestingly the term guilt and its derivatives occur 145 times in the Old Testament and 10 times in the New Testament, whereas the term "shame" and its derivatives occur nearly 300 times in the Old Testament and 45 in the New Testament[ix]. The Bible was largely written in a different worldview, the majority worldview of honour/shame.

Eugene Nida wrote in Customs and Cultures *"We have to reckon with three different types of reactions to transgressions of religiously sanctioned codes: fear, shame, and guilt."* Missiologists have identified 3 cultural worldviews that show our need of the Gospel.

i)   Innocence / Guilt

ii)   Honour / Shame

iii)   Power / Fear

Each of them deals with the effects of sin from different points of view, shaped by the different cultures and worldviews prevalent in the world. Our sin makes us guilty, brings us shame, or causes fear of the spirit world. Jesus' death on the cross deals with our guilt, so we are declared not guilty and indeed righteous. It takes away our shame and restores us to the place of honour. Jesus is the man of power who takes away fear of evil powers by winning the victory over them for us. The Bible is incredible – it has power to reach every culture and has the good news in understandable ways for every culture.

Each one of those worldviews has counterfeit ways of trying to achieve the positive. Each one is addressed by the Gospel, the good news of Jesus death on the cross and resurrection to bring us into relationship with the Father.

Innocence/Guilt

In innocence/guilt cultures people try to earn their favour from God by their own works and righteous acts. Isaiah 64:6 tells us that *our righteous acts are like a polluted cloth*. Literally a used menstrual cloth. The gospel tells us *"For by grace you have been saved by faith. And this is not your own doing; it is the gift of God, not a result of works so that no one may boast." Eph 2:8.*

Honour/Shame

In honour/shame cultures people work for achieved honour. Honour is the sense of worth or value people have in their own eyes and in the eyes of their community. Jesus told a story of a wedding feast in Luke 14:7-11. In it he tells his listeners

"Do not sit down in the place of honour, lest someone more distinguished than you be invited by him and he who invited you both will come and say to you 'Give your place to this person' and then you will begin with shame to take the lowest place. But when you are invited, go and sit in the lowest place, so that when your host comes he may say to you, 'Friend, move up higher.' Then you will be honoured in the presence of all who sit at table with you."

In those short verses, Jesus deals with two types of honour. Achieved honour is honour in the eyes of those around you by what you have done. Sitting at top table is going for achieved honour, which generally results in shame from overstepping and missing the mark. Ascribed honour is honour that is bestowed upon you.

> He treated everyone with honour and dignity, undermining society's sense of false honour.

The gospel in honour/shame cultures starts with God who has always existed with ultimate honour and glory. He created the earth to display his glory with the pinnacle of creation as mankind. They co-ruled the world with honour. Adam and Eve were disloyal to God, disobeying him, bringing shame on themselves by their sin. What is the emotion they felt when they blew it? Guilt, Fear or Shame? All three! But primarily expressed in Genesis 3 as shame *"they knew they were naked"* v7 and fear *"I was afraid"* v10. All mankind inherits that same shame for sin that Adam and Eve experienced. Sin is trying to gain honour and cover shame.

In 2013 two brothers committed a terrorist atrocity at the Boston Marathon. In a press conference their uncle, Ruslan Tsarni, begged his nephew to turn himself and ask for forgiveness. He stated that he had brought shame on the family and the entire Chechen ethnicity, who will be seen as terrorists[x]. Shame for sin is a community thing and consequently a much deeper experienced emotion than individualistic guilt.

Jesus was seated at the right hand of the Father in the ultimate place of honour. He humbled himself, becoming a man to save people from shame and bring them back to the place of honour. He treated everyone with honour and dignity, undermining society's sense of false honour.

The religious leaders hated that and shamed him publicly in the ultimate way by crucifying him on a cross. He endured the shame and the pain of that cruel death. God the Father raised him from the dead and restored him to His right hand, with a name higher than any other.

People who follow Jesus are given a new dignity and honour, shame is taken away. They need to renounce face saving and honour grabbing and trust Jesus for their new status. Christians are able to honour others and when Jesus returns, non-believers will be banished forever, while believers will receive crowns of glory and honour forever in God's presence.

Power/Fear

The power /fear paradigm abounds in animistic tribal cultures where people are afraid of evil and pursue the power of the spirit world through magic rituals. Jesus, the ultimate man of power, disarmed the principalities and powers on the cross (Col 2:15) and takes away fear through his perfect love (1 John 4:7).

The power/fear narrative starts with God who created the heavens and earth by His powerful word. He rules with absolute power benevolently. Adam was created to reign over the earth with God. Some of the angels rebelled against God. Satan illegitimately used the serpent to trick humanity to coming under his power. He is the prince of the world who has blinded humanity to God's goodness and ultimate power. Jesus is God's power incarnated. He resisted Satan's offer of co-ruling and showed God's power by healing the sick, raising the dead and setting people free from Satan's power. Satan counterattacked having Jesus put to death on the cross. That backfired because the cross and resurrection disarmed the principalities and powers. People must turn from the dark powers to Jesus and follow Him. God blesses Christians with every spiritual blessing and the same power of the Spirit that raised Jesus from the dead enabling them to resist the devil and rendering black magic and occult power powerless. At the end of time God will bind Satan and his demons permanently and reign with His followers forever more on a new heaven and a new earth.

What is your cultural background?

There is a culture test online to work out which cultural paradigm – guilt, shame or fear you are living in at theculturetest.com/survey. I came out 84% innocence/guilt, 12% honour/shame and 4% power/fear. It just shows how cultures have mixed. I have noticed shame growing in the UK context alongside the growth of social media and the infiltration of moral relativism. People are less concerned with absolute right and wrong, but they do feel shamed when they have transgressed the right and wrong they don't believe in anymore and are embarrassed in public!

These three gospel paradigms are all completely Scriptural and because they are cultural, you may have missed them completely because of the cultural spectacle we are wearing as we read the Bible. As I have begun to have my eyes opened it has increased my grasp of the wonder of the Gospel.

The Apostle Paul wrote the book of Ephesians to explain *"the unsearchable riches of Christ"* Eph 3:8. In it he tackles each of three paradigms. Guilt/innocence is sorted because *"In him we have redemption through His blood, the forgiveness of our trespasses, according to the riches of His grace."* 1:7 and the fact that *"even when we were dead in our trespasses, (we are) made alive together with Christ."* Eph 2:5 Honour/shame is dealt with Eph 1:5 where we are adopted as sons and made fellow citizens Eph 2:19. Power/fear is tackled in Eph 1:19-21 *and what is the immeasurable greatness of his power toward us who believe, according to the working of his great might that he worked in Christ when he raised him from the dead and seated him at his right hand in the heavenly places, far above all rule and authority and power and dominion, and above every name that is named, not only in this age but also in the one to come.*

It is so enriching to begin to read the Bible 3-Dimensionally as Jayson Georges puts it in "3D Gospel". It allows us *"to grasp the riches of His grace, that he lavished upon us with all wisdom and insight"* Eph 1:7-8.

Crossing the line of faith

How does this affect helping someone cross the line of faith? Most people live their lives not realising they are guilty before a holy God, or living in shame because of their sin or in fear of the spirit world. When talking about spiritual matters one of those three will connect better than the others.

When I lead some Asians girls to the Lord, I used the Bridge to Life diagram, which is firmly based in the innocence/guilt paradigm. When I recounted the story to missiologist Liz Hentschel, she laughed, "They would never have understood that!" But by the grace of God and the power of the Spirit, they did! But it did make me want to be more culturally aware of how I share the good news to people.

> Guilt tells us "I made a mistake", whereas shame shouts to us "I am a mistake".

I'll never forget the response of a young lady originally from the Caribbean to a gospel sermon from an honour/shame perspective. She said "I have been a Christian for years, knowing I was forgiven, but I have always felt ashamed. Now I am free." Guilt tells us "I made a mistake", whereas shame shouts to us "I am a mistake". It is a far more devastating and powerful emotion. Friends from shame cultures need to know that the Gospel takes away shame and restores them to a place of honour before the Father.

As I am chatting to someone, I'm listening to them and the Spirit, looking for which paradigm is going to make most sense to the person. Guilt / Innocence is mainly a Western paradigm. Honour /

Shame is typically Eastern and Power / Fear is the worldview of tribal people groups.

Every cultural paradigm has a way of explaining the four key elements of the Gospel - Creation, Fall, Jesus, Restoration.

God created a perfect world, the fall marred it and people through sin. Jesus came to bring us into relationship with God and one day He will return to restore the earth and dwell with us for ever.

Innocence/Guilt

Creation: God created the world and mankind for relationship with Him. We were created to rule with him with only one rule: to not eat from the tree of the knowledge of good and evil

Fall: People are sinful and this creates a barrier between us and God

Jesus: is the perfect sacrifice for our sins. He died on the cross in our place to pay the penalty for our sin.

Restoration: if we trust in Jesus as our Lord and Saviour we are declared not guilty and righteous and will get to enjoy eternal life with Him forever.

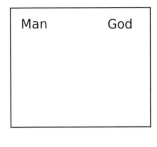

I most often express this using the Bridge to Life™ scribbled on a scrap of paper. When I get to this point in a conversation and friendship I'd ask if I could explain my faith with a picture.

I start off by writing God on the right hand side and Man on the left and explaining that God loves us and we were created to be friends with God.

Right at the start, Adam and Eve were told they could do anything they like except one thing – eat from the tree of the knowledge of good and evil. What do you think they did? Yes they did the one thing they shouldn't. They rebelled against God and brought evil into the world.

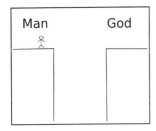

Ever since then we are all the same – we all do things wrong, say things wrong and think things that are wrong and that has separated us from God, breaking the relationship we once had. *At this point I draw in the chasm.*

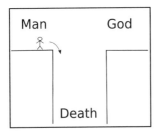

We are all aware of that separation and many of us will try and do things to bridge the gap – being nice to people, helping old ladies across the road, maybe even going to church. All good stuff but the Bible makes it clear we can't do anything to bridge the gap or earn God's forgiveness. *I'll draw in an arrow and then write death at the bottom.* I'll usually explain that Romans 6:23 tells us that the wages of sin is death.

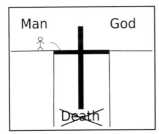

It's a bleak picture and not one that God wants. God loves us so he did what we can't do. He bridged the gap from His side, so that we can find forgiveness and a relationship with God. He did it by sending Jesus to come to the world to be like us and die on the cross. for our sin. *At that point I'll draw the cross bridging the gap and cross out death.* If I have a Bible with me (and I usually do have a pocket one with me!), I'll probably point to 1 Peter 3:18 "For Christ also suffered once for sins, the righteous for the unrighteous, that he might bring us to God."

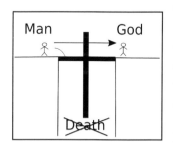

Then finally I'll draw another stick man on the God side and explain that by admitting we have rebelled against God and asking Jesus to forgive us and lead us means that we can be forgiven and enjoy a relationship with God.

I'll ask if there is anything they didn't understand. I will explain further if necessary. Then I ask them to point where they are on the diagram and whether they would like to move over the bridge by asking Jesus to be their forgiver and Lord.

Sometimes they are ready and other times they need to think about it or count the cost further.

Honour / Shame

Creation: God created mankind with honour and dignity to live as family with Him.

Fall: People are sinful and commit shameful acts dishonouring God. Our attempts to gain honour fall short and only increase our sense of shame.

Jesus: His disgraceful death on the cross bore our shame and restores honour. By honouring Jesus we are restored to a new place of honour and our shame is taken away.

Restoration: We must pledge our allegiance to Jesus and receive God's gracious welcome and honour. Stop trying to gain false honour.

People from an honour/shame culture are used to storytelling. What better story to use than one from the master storyteller Jesus? For me the ultimate honour / shame story is the parable of the prodigal son.

And he said, "There was a man who had two sons. And the younger of them said to his father, 'Father, give me the share of property that is coming to me.' And he divided his property between them. Not many days later, the younger son gathered all he had and took a journey into a far country, and there he squandered his property in reckless living. And when he had spent everything, a severe famine arose in that country, and he began to be in need. So he went and hired himself out to one of the citizens of that country, who sent him into his fields to feed pigs. And he was longing to be fed with the pods that the pigs ate, and no one gave him anything.

"But when he came to himself, he said, 'How many of my father's hired servants have more than enough bread, but I perish here with hunger! I will arise and go to my father, and I will say to him, "Father, I have sinned against heaven and before you. I am no longer worthy to be called your son. Treat me as one of your hired servants."' And he arose and came to his father. But while he was still a long way off, his father saw him and felt compassion, and ran and embraced him and kissed him. And the son said to him, 'Father, I have sinned against heaven and before you. I am no longer worthy to be called your son.' But

113

the father said to his servants, 'Bring quickly the best robe, and put it on him, and put a ring on his hand, and shoes on his feet. And bring the fattened calf and kill it, and let us eat and celebrate. For this my son was dead, and is alive again; he was lost, and is found.' And they began to celebrate. Luke 15:11-24

I'd tell the story something like this...

There was once a honourable, well off family – a father and two sons. Two sons start off greatly honoured. The younger son wanted his inheritance now – which brought great shame on Father because he was effectively saying "I want you dead now!"

He goes off, living like a fool, bringing shame on himself with wine, women and song. Eventually the money runs out, just as famine comes. He is faced with the consequences. Romans 1 expresses the wrath of God as Him giving the sinner over to what they desire, including the consequences

So the young man hires himself to feed pigs, which in Jewish culture are unclean animals. That's heightened shame – he really knows the depth of shame he is under.

This young man, who was once proud, is now humbled. He wakes up and realises foolishness. He wants to earn way out of shame. He comes up with a plan to return, repent and be a slave. He is no longer worthy of honour.

So he starts back. As he enters the other end of the village, the Father sees him and comes running to embrace him and kiss him. It was shameful to run as an adult. Father shames himself to cover the Son's shame. This loving Father, full of compassion – is protecting the son from shameful walk through the village.

114

The story is told in Spain of a father and his teenage son who had a relationship that had become strained. So the son ran away from home. His father however, began a journey in search of his rebellious son. Finally, in Madrid, in a last desperate effort to find him, the father put an advert in the newspaper. It read: "Dear Paco, meet me in front of the newspaper office at noon tomorrow. All is forgiven. I love you. Your father" The next day at noon in front of the newspaper office 800 "Pacos" showed up. They were all seeking forgiveness and love from their fathers.

The younger son was brought low, he realised the shame of his sin - turned in repentance to the Father and had his honour restored and shame taken away.

I'd then ask if they want victory over sin and shame? If they want the honour of being a child of God. If they do I would lead them in a prayer of turning to Jesus to receive honour and shame cleansed.

Power/Fear

Creation: God is sovereign and created mankind to rule His creation (both seen and unseen) with Him.

Fall: We fell under Satan's trickery to live under his power. Sin, death and harm are the results of his rule.

Jesus: He conquered evil with his power and authority. His death disarmed the principalities and powers and enables us to live under His blessing.

Restoration: When we trust Jesus we receive His power and protection.

I have not yet explained the gospel from someone from a power/fear culture, but when I do I won't be talking about Jesus meek and mild! He is the warrior king who disarmed the principalities and powers making a spectacle of them.

As you can see, this triple worldview of guilt, shame and fear are a powerful cocktail for reaching every culture. But the reality is that we are all a mix. Earlier in the chapter I shared my results of doing the "Culture test" 84% guilt, 12% shame, 4% fear. The fact is that we can be saved from guilt and still live in shame of the things we have done and in fear of what's out there. We may not see that fear spiritually, analysing it as the credit crunch, terrorism or relationship issues. Grasping how the gospel deals with innocence/guilt, honour/shame and power/fear will help you grasp the goodness and kindness of God and make you more effective helping others cross the line of faith into a relationship with the Father.

With each cultural viewpoint there is a point where a person recognises their need of Jesus to take away guilt, shame or fear and restore relationship with God in innocence, honour or power.

I ask them where they are at with what I have said. On the bridge to life I'd ask them to point where they are at on the diagram. Then I ask them if they would like to cross the line from one to the other.

I explain that we do it with a simple prayer – talking out loud to God trusting that He loves us and listens to us. Sometimes people prefer to follow along a prayer I pray line by line, others just needs some pointers along the way. Either way I am looking for them to trust Jesus to save them from guilt, shame and fear and bring them into forgiveness, honour and the power of knowing God.

Celebrate when they have done it. Romans 10:9 tells us that if *"you confess with your mouth that Jesus is Lord and believe in your heart that God raised him from the dead you will be saved."*

After we have prayed together, I encourage them to tell someone as soon as possible to seal the deal! Then I am looking to see them filled with the power of the Spirit through the baptism in Spirit.

Application

1) Take the culture test to work out which cultural paradigm you are in.

2) Prepare how you would share the gospel with a friend from

    i)   Guilt/innocence culture

    ii)   Honour/shame culture

    iii)   Power/Fear culture

Look for an opportunity this week.

11

Leading someone into the baptism in Spirit

And he said to them, "Did you receive the Holy Spirit when you believed?" And they said, "No, we have not even heard that there is a Holy Spirit." (Acts 19:2 ESV)

We saw earlier that becoming a disciple involves four things – repentance, faith, baptism in water and baptism in Spirit. Repentance and faith were covered in the last chapter. This chapter covers baptism in Spirit.

Church history hinges on one verse – Acts 1:8 "You shall receive power when the Holy Spirit comes upon you". It changed weak men into world changers. So it is vital to lead new disciples into an experience of being filled with the power of the Holy Spirit.

Terry Virgo, the founding father of the Newfrontiers family of churches has been so helpful on how to lead people through into the baptism in the Spirit. His advice is that we take people through the scriptures in Acts to show and build faith for the experience.

None of the Epistles command baptism in water or the Spirit – it's just taken for granted, because they are letters written to established churches. The book of Acts shows us the history of churches getting planted and disciples being made.

Acts 2:38 *And Peter said to them "Repent and be baptised every one of you in the name of Jesus Christ for the forgiveness of your sins, and you will receive the gift of the Holy Spirit. For the promise is for you and for your children and all who are far off, everyone whom the Lord calls to himself."*

The initial 120 were already believers, disciples of Jesus who were then filled with the Spirit at Pentecost and spoke in tongues, resulting in 3000 more saved and added to the church.

> *Acts 8:12-16 But when they believed Philip as he preached good news about the kingdom of God and the name of Jesus Christ, they were baptized, both men and women. Even Simon himself believed, and after being baptized he continued with Philip. And seeing signs and great miracles performed, he was amazed.*
>
> *Now when the apostles at Jerusalem heard that Samaria had received the word of God, they sent to them Peter and John, who came down and prayed for them that they might receive the Holy Spirit, for he had not yet fallen on any of them, but they had only been baptized in the name of the Lord Jesus. Then they laid their hands on them and they received the Holy Spirit.*

Here the Samaritans hear the Gospel, respond with repentance, faith and baptism in water. Later Peter and John come and make sure the fourth leg is in place by praying for them to receive the baptism in the Spirit.

Acts 10:44-46 While Peter was still saying these things, the Holy Spirit fell on all who heard the word. And the believers from among the circumcised who had come with Peter were amazed, because the gift of the Holy Spirit was poured out even on the Gentiles. For they were hearing them speaking in tongues and extolling God. Then Peter declared, "Can anyone withhold water for baptizing these people, who have received the Holy Spirit just as we have?" And he commanded them to be baptized in the name of Jesus Christ. Then they asked him to remain for some days.

The Spirit fell on a group of Gentiles listening to Peter preach sovereignly. I think at this point none of the Jewish believers would have laid hands by touch, so God just does it. They receive tongues and praise as outward manifestations.

> *Acts 19:2-6 And he said to them, "Did you receive the Holy Spirit when you believed?" And they said, "No, we have not even heard that there is a Holy Spirit." And he said, "Into what then were you baptized?" They said, "Into John's baptism." And Paul said, "John baptized with the baptism of repentance, telling the people to believe in the one who was to come after him, that is, Jesus." On hearing this, they were baptized in the name of the Lord Jesus. And when Paul had laid his hands on them, the Holy Spirit came on them, and they began speaking in tongues and prophesying. There were about twelve men in all.*

When Paul reached Ephesus he asked the group there whether they had been baptised in the Spirit. The answer showed him they hadn't received the gospel either! So he sorted out all four legs and they receive tongues and or prophecy as the outward manifestation.

These scriptures build up evidence that three of the four traditional views are weak.

Evangelical – already have it automatically is refuted by the question Paul asked in Acts 19 and the fact that the Holy Spirit hadn't fallen on them in Acts 8.

Second Blessing – Cornelius was pretty quick! As was Paul and the Ephesians

Pentecostal tarrying – only the initial disciples had to tarry in the city until the Spirit came at Pentecost. Now He is freely available to all who are thirsty and come for a drink!

On the last day of the feast, the great day, Jesus stood up and cried out, "If anyone thirsts, let him come to me and drink. Whoever believes in me, as the Scripture has said, 'Out of his heart will flow rivers of living water.'" Now this he said about the Spirit, whom those who believed in him were to receive, for as yet the Spirit had not been given, because Jesus was not yet glorified. John 7:37-39

That statement is a prophetic word when Jesus gave it, as the Spirit had been given at that point, but now He is glorified we don't need to wait – the Spirit is available for us now!

There are three essentials to be baptised in the Spirit

i)   **Be thirsty**   you don't need to be a mature Christian or attain a level of holiness first. In Gal. 3:2 Paul asks *"Let me ask you only this: Did you receive the Spirit by works of the law or by hearing with faith?"* We come by faith not our efforts.

ii)   **Come** – when we invite people to be prayed for, we are inviting them to come to Jesus to receive. Whether you are being prayed for by Paul, Peter, John or little old me, you are coming to Jesus.

iii)   **Drink** – Come and drink. He has promised to give the Spirit to those who ask so we must come believing that He will give.

In the Acts examples, many of them tell us "they spoke in tongues." Not all, but most of them. Tongues is such a helpful gift to build us up, that I'm looking for people to receive it when I pray for the baptism in the Spirit.

God doesn't do it, we do it by faith! We have to open our mouths and speak by faith! 1 Corinthians 14 tells us our minds our unfruitful when we speak in tongues – we can think about other things, including "Am I making this up?!" Studies have been done showing that the language centres of the brain are less active when people are speaking in tongues, with their spirit, than when they pray with their mind. When I am praying for people to receive and encouraging them to speak out I remind them that their minds aren't involved, so if they are doubting it is real, that's a kind of evidence it is real!

We don't receive the gift of tongues passively. When Peter was called by Jesus out of the boat, he had to step out of the boat! He had to use his feet in another dimension. When we receive the gift of tongues we are using our lungs, voice box and mouths in another spiritual dimension too! We don't stand and wait for God, we speak by faith!

Take time to build faith for receiving the gift of tongues from the Scriptures. Faith that is biblically rooted is so much stronger.

Once I have explained the Scriptures and the person is ready we come to Jesus, pray over them to be filled and impart the gift of tongues expecting them to speak!

Going through Scriptures has built Biblical faith and so for most the start speaking in tongues straight away. Some need to do it in the privacy of their own homes later – I've noticed lots of shy people do that!

Application

1) Have you been baptised in the Spirit? If not having read this chapter ask Jesus to fill you right now and speak in tongues or get a friend to pray with you.

2) Do a small group evening on the baptism in the Spirit to bring people through.

12

Conclusion

After this I looked, and behold, a great multitude that no one could number, from every nation, from all tribes and peoples and languages, standing before the throne and before the Lamb, clothed in white robes, with palm branches in their hands, and crying out with a loud voice, "Salvation belongs to our God who sits on the throne, and to the Lamb!" (Revelation 7:9-10 ESV)

I am longing for that day when we get to stand before Jesus at the wedding feast of the Lamb. We will be able to look around and see people who we have had an eternal impact on. People we have befriended. People we have eaten with. People that we have shared something of the Gospel with. There will be some surprises. Some friends who we thought had never responded or never shown any interest, who took the Gospel into their hearts. Some others, we knew for a while, who moved on before they became a disciple and crossed the line of faith somewhere else.

Looking forward to friends being with me in eternity is a powerful motivator for me to do Friends, Food and the Gospel. The second and probably greater motivator is the love of God that has been shed abroad in my heart and overflows.

In Paul's second letter to the Corinthians, he wrote:

For the love of Christ controls us, because we have concluded this: that one has died for all, therefore all have died; and he died for all, that those who live might no longer live for themselves but for him who for their sake died and was raised. (2 Corinthians 5:14-15 ESV)

It's that powerful encounter with God's love, in the Gospel, that controls us or as the NIV puts it "compels us". The Gospel has so transformed us with the love, goodness and kindness of God that we no longer live for ourselves but for Him.

That love spills over to those around us, who we count as friends and those we look to befriend. Those we befriend we eat with, because that's what friends too. Then what is in our hearts overflows as we share the good news we have found.

Friends, food and the Gospel.

I'd like to finish with Allesio's story and a challenge to create your own.

When I first came to King's Lynn, earlier last year, I was at a turning point in my life. Having just graduated from medical school back in Italy, it was time to start work. That for me meant moving abroad, leaving family and friends behind. I don't think I could have ever imagined what the biggest change in my life would have been, if somebody asked me when I first arrived.

There were times at first when it was easy to feel lonely and discouraged, far away from anybody I could call a friend, and being thrown into a very demanding job which I didn't really feel prepared for. Everything truly changed when I met the people I now consider my second family, in King's Lynn.

It all started with a co-worker asking about my spiritual life. It was brave of her and I thank God today for it! We used to talk over lunch about religion, what our views were on the matter, just exchanging thoughts without judging on either part. On my side, I grew up in a Christian family, and despite being very involved in church from a young age, when I left for university I put it all aside. At some point I thought that was something I didn't need in my life.

Back to our story, I was invited to her church, and I'm not one to say no to the chance of meeting new people, so I went.

The people I met there were by far the most generous, friendly and genuinely good people I've ever met. Everybody was working hard to glorify God in the way that best suited them. Some by singing or playing instruments, others with their ever so present words of encouragement or ever-ready listening ear. Coming from Italy, I had no other choice than to cook for people.

And that's when it started. We have had many evenings of laughter, fun and games, alternating with serious moments of reflection, listening to each other's problems and praying together. Many of our nights centred around meals, because that is something that always bring people together, and I believe it much more now, having experienced that for myself. Putting your skills at God's service, whatever they are, is something that will always bring you happiness and satisfaction.

With the months gone by, I saw so many changes in my life. First came all the new friends and relationships with awesome people. Then I started to feel the presence of God beside me, in my everyday life and often times at work. And now, working as a doctor, I think that's an invaluable thing to have. So many people are in need of the comfort that only He can give, especially when they're ill or facing death.

I recognise now that God has never abandoned me, even when I turned my back to Him. He had a plan for me that is now starting to unravel, and I can't wait to find out what He has planned next!

Appendix 1 How many do you know?

Here's a list of the top 100 UK surnames[xi], how many people do you know with them? Off the top of my head I came up with 124 - most people can think of 20 or so, but connectors will know hundreds

Smith		Wood		Mitchell		Webb	
Jones		Turner		Kelly		Rogers	
Williams		Martin		Cook		Gray	
Taylor		Cooper		Carter		Mason	
Brown		Hill		Richardson		Ali	
Davies		Ward		Bailey		Hunt	
Evans		Morris		Collins		Hussain	
Wilson		Moore		Bell		Campbell	
Thomas		Clark		Shaw		Matthews	
Johnson		Lee		Murphy		Owen	
Roberts		King		Miller		Palmer	
Robinson		Baker		Cox		Holmes	
Thompson		Harrison		Richards		Mills	
Wright		Morgan		Khan		Barnes	
Walker		Allen		Marshall		Knight	

White		James		Anderson		Lloyd	
Edwards		Scott		Simpson		Butler	
Hughes		Phillips		Ellis		Russell	
Green		Watson		Adams		Barker	
Hall		Davis		Singh		Fisher	
Lewis		Parker		Begum		Stevens	
Harris		Price		Wilkinson		Jenkins	
Clarke		Bennett		Foster		Murray	
Patel		Young		Chapman		Dixon	
Jackson		Griffiths		Powell		Harvey	

The higher the number of people you know with those surname, the more likely it is that you are wired to be a Connector.

Other Reading

Becoming a Contagious Christian
Bill Hybels & Mark Mittelburg
1998 Zondervan
http://amzn.to/2atxch3

Dining in the Kingdom of God
Eugene La Verdiere
1994 Archdiocese of Chicago
http://amzn.to/2atwXT2

A Meal with Jesus
Tim Chester
2011 IVP Press
http://amzn.to/2atx54Y

THE 3D GOSPEL: Ministry in Guilt, Shame, and Fear Cultures
Jayson Georges
2014 Time Press
http://amzn.to/2ah1fFs

The Normal Christian Birth
David Pawson
1989 Hodder and Stoughton
http://amzn.to/2ah1iRs

Tipping Point
Malcolm Gladwell
2002 Abacus
http://amzn.to/2dXOgh1

Scripture References

References

[i] Meals with Jesus, Tim Chester, published by IVP

[ii] http://news.bbc.co.uk/1/shared/bsp/hi/pdfs/03_04_07_tearfundchurch.pdf

[iii] http://www.ethnicharvest.org/links/articles/bridges_man_of_peace.htm

[iv] http://www.transformationchurch.tc/sermons/index.php?GIGQ/how_treat_muslims/

[v] http://www.telegraph.co.uk/news/uknews/11026520/Lonely-Britain-five-million-people-who-have-no-real-friends.html

[vi] https://newchurches.com/episode-102-maximizing-community-events-and-engagement/ accessed 14th Sept 2016

[vii] http://www.knoxpriest.com/scruffy-hospitality-creates-space-friendship/

[viii] http://www.knoxpriest.com/scruffy-hospitality-creates-space-friendship/

[ix] The Global Gospel by Werner Mischke, published by Mission One Resources

[x] Interview on http://www.bbc.co.uk/news/world-us-canada-22223015

[xi] http://surnames.behindthename.com/top/lists/england-wales/1991